SIR JOHN SUMMERSON is Curator of Sir John Soane's Museum, London. He is a Fellow of the British Academy, a Fellow of the Society of Antiquaries, and an Associate of the Royal Institute of British Architects. His teaching posts have included Slade Professor of Fine Art at Oxford, 1958-1959, and Ferens Professor of Fine Art at the University of Hull, 1960-1961. Sir John is the author of *Architecture in Britain, 1530-1830, Architecture Here and Now, Georgian London,* and other books; his *Heavenly Mansions and Other Essays on Architecture* and *Victorian Architecture in England* are both published in Norton Library editions.

VICTORIAN ARCHITECTURE IN ENGLAND

Four Studies in Evaluation

by JOHN SUMMERSON

The Norton Library

W · W · NORTON & COMPANY · INC ·
NEW YORK

Preface

THE FOUR LECTURES contained in this book were prepared at the invitation of Columbia University, New York, and delivered as the Bampton Lectures for 1968 in March of that year. Apart from factual corrections and occasional second thoughts they are printed here as spoken. In offering them in this form I would like to express deep appreciation of my appointment as Bampton Lecturer as well as to acknowledge the University's generous hospitality in New York. To which I would add my most cordial thanks to Professor and Mrs. Rudolf Wittkower for their warm interest and kindness to my wife and me throughout our visit.

London, England: March, 1969   John Summerson

Contents

VICTORIAN ARCHITECTURE IN ENGLAND   Four Studies in Evaluation

I. The Evaluation of Victorian Architecture: The Problem of Failure

I HAVE CHOSEN for my subject the evaluation of Victorian architecture because it seems to me that there is a problem here which does not exist in other areas of architectural history. The essence of the problem is this: We are accustomed to assess buildings, groups of buildings, episodes, schools of architecture on the assumption that whether they have or have not for us an immediate relevance or emotional appeal they were at least in their time accepted as right. On that basis we begin to evaluate. We discover the sources of influence and the main agents of stylistic change. We are able to distinguish the major from the minor work, the minor from the merely derivative. The contents of the area we are considering assume a certain shape and outline in which, however much in detail it may be subject to controversy, we have confidence. We know, of course, that this outline is not all. We know that if we look carefully enough we shall find within it the seeds of self-destruction, anticipatory twists of revolution. Nevertheless, we pass in our minds an Act of Settlement in respect of the entire situation with which we are concerned.

Now in the case of Victorian architecture, I do not believe that any such Act of Settlement is at present possible. One often stated reason has been that we are "too near" the Victorians to view them in proper perspective, though I am bound to say that the elasticity of "too-nearness" is getting rather strained, at least where early and mid-Victorianism is concerned, and it is early and mid-Victorianism with which I shall be dealing. Another reason—and, I think, the real one—is our failure to appreciate that early and mid-Victorian architecture was, in its own time and in the eyes of its own best-informed critics, horribly unsuccessful. I said just now that we are accustomed to begin evaluating the contents of a period of architecture on the assumption that in relation to the society which built, it was right. Where the Victorians are concerned it would be very much safer to begin, at least, on the assumption that it was wrong.

An older generation, only just extinct, took this as axiomatic. Exactly at the end of Victoria's reign it was finally concluded everywhere that earlier Victorian architecture was bad architecture. G. K. Chesterton witnessed this decision taken and wrote in 1904: "There is no more remarkable psychological element in history than the way in which a period can suddenly become unintelligible. To the early Victorian period we have in a moment lost the key: the Crystal Palace is the temple of a forgotten creed. The thing always happens sharply: a whisper runs through the Salons, Mr. Max Beerbohm waves a wand and a whole generation of great men and great achievement suddenly looks mildewed and unmeaning."[1] Unintelligible; and not only unintelligible but absolutely bad. The historian G. M. Trevelyan, born in 1876, was of Chesterton's generation and he, in his best-selling *English Social History,* published in 1942, disposed of Victorian architecture like this:

These grandfathers and great-grandfathers of ours, though they compassed sea and land to admire Roman acqueducts and Gothic cathedrals, themselves produced deplorable buildings. . . . The most refined and educated classes were as bad as any: the monstrosities of architecture erected by order of the Dons of Oxford and Cambridge colleges in the days of William Butterfield and Alfred Waterhouse give daily pain to posterity.[2]

THE EVALUATION OF
VICTORIAN
ARCHITECTURE

2

He goes on to blame Ruskin, jerry-building, the Industrial

Revolution, and mass production; which makes it clear that Trevelyan, a grand historian in his way, had never thought seriously about Victorian architecture and was simply voicing the conviction of his generation that in architecture the Victorians had failed. That was the point of view which my own generation inherited. I was sent in 1918 to a public school which, having risen to fame as a rival to Eton in the earlier part of the century, was particularly well endowed with Victorian buildings. Cockerell, Donaldson, Scott, Burges, Hayward, Jackson, Champneys, Prior were all well represented. Cockerell escaped criticism because his work, based in this rare instance on Tudor prototypes, was believed to be the genuine article and in fact the work of the school's founder in the reign of the first Elizabeth. For Scott, Burges, and Hayward no reprobation could be too severe. "They belong," said the art master, exercising the full weight of his unique authority, "to the worst period of the Gothic Revival." And that was that. To Jackson, Champneys, and Prior, whose buildings had been built after "the worst period" and, indeed, within the living memory of some, our masters were a little kinder; and when a red-brick Renaissance house by Jackson was torn down to make room for an expensive war memorial by Baker there were even murmurs of regret. One was left in no doubt where "the worst period" lay—1870 was the year most often stigmatized—and about the proper attitude to be taken to it.

I quote my own youthful experience here because it represents the common experience of my generation and explains to some extent that generation's later somewhat cautious approach to the revaluation of Victorian architecture. Nevertheless revaluation has long been in the air. In the arts, as in morals, if a schoolboy is told that something is bad he involuntarily pursues it, and my own curiosity about Victorian architecture began forty-five years ago with the *frisson* induced by having the horrors of Scott's chapel and library and Burges's speech-room at Harrow daily before my eyes. Their hard profiles and garish polychromy I followed my elders in detesting, and I accepted that they were "bad." But it did from time to time occur to me that the men who had built them were not exactly fools. The floriated hinges of the library doors, the intricate flèche of the chapel, and some drawings by Burges in the school museum seemed to prove the contrary. Without actually surrendering to these things, the seeds of curiosity were by them implanted.

It is important to establish the utter revulsion against Victorian architecture which existed in those days but perhaps even more important to try to discover its sources. The easy explanation is that it was the natural reaction of one generation against the works of its predecessor. But this will not do. Generations do not always react with this intensity. In the eight generations between Brunelleschi and Guarini, in the seven generations between Inigo Jones and Soane, there were indeed many revolutions in taste and ideas but nothing in any way comparable to the complete severance of communication which, as Chesterton bears witness, took place at the end of Victoria's reign between the people of that time and the works of their fathers before 1870. It is this absolute severance of communication and its consequences which sets us our problem and makes the modern evaluation of early and mid-Victorian things so curiously difficult.

The explanation, I believe, of this severance lies in this. Victorian architecture up to 1870 *was*, as I have already suggested, a failure. It was felt by many at the time to be a failure, declared by some to be a failure, and received by the next generation as a failure, duly accepted and declared. When Trevelyan, writing in 1942, described Victorian architecture as "deplorable" and its works as "monstrosities," he was not, I am sure, giving expression to any considered estimate of his own; he was echoing exactly the opinions he would have received as an undergraduate, the opinions of men who in their youth had shuddered at Street's new Law Courts and howled derision at Scott's St. Pancras Hotel. In other words, the failure of Victorian architecture was already recognized in the seventies, fully confirmed by 1900, and passed on as axiomatic to a generation which as it grew up began to wonder, in its idler moments, whether this estimate was correct or, in other terms, what "failure" in such a context could possibly mean. No modern writer that I know of has given an entirely adequate answer.

I have said that Victorian architecture up to 1870 was a failure, a statement which, I realize, requires the production of a certain amount of supporting evidence. Is it possible, you may well ask, to characterize any period in the history of art as a "failure" or indeed as a "success" and if so what are the tests? Clearly, I must be more explicit. You will agree, of course, that if we are trying to assess the achievements of any period of building activity we must take into consideration all that the period contains and not merely a few outstanding works which fascinate by their strangeness or luxuriance. We must look at the architects, their groupings, their individual and collective ideas and loyalties. We must look at the workings of patronage, the stresses of religion, and social class. On all these factors, where Victorian architecture is concerned, there is a great mass of evidence, to the extent that by careful selection almost any verdict could be arrived at. There is, nevertheless, at least in my reading of the evidence, one recurring element which cannot be missed, which colors the evidence wherever one looks, and that element is—doubt.

The conception of the Victorian age as the age of doubt is, of course, familiar—crucially in the sphere of religious belief. But doubt and anxiety spread far beyond this, and whenever the Victorian attitude is most earnest and assured we soon find that those qualities are the outward, visible, and defensive manifestation of profound anxiety. This was well summarized in a short essay of 1948 by the late Humphry House:

The more I read of the early- and mid-Victorians, the more I see anxiety and worry as a leading clue to understanding them. They were not complacent compromisers. They were trying to hold together incompatible opposites, and they worried because they failed. They clung to an immortality that should not include the justice of Eternal Punishment; they wanted a system of administration which should be efficient without expense; in face of repeated and ferocious strikes and riots they clung to the doctrine that the interests of employers and employed were identical. They knew such things as these were incompatibles. They worried because they could neither reconcile them nor move on to other terms of thought. They worried about immortality, they worried about sex, they worried about politics and money. They were indeed caught between two worlds.[8]

And they worried, too, about architecture. That they worried about architecture is obvious to anyone having the slightest acquaintance with the history of the profession up to 1870, a period which saw not only the institution of the most significant professional bodies but also the development of a most diligent and fertile professional press. Worry does not necessarily lead to failure; it may be resolved in triumphant success. But my contention here is that the ambiguities in the Victorian conception of architecture were so profound that for some three decades no building could escape their tortion, and that in our present-day enthusiasm for reinstating and revaluing a lost epoch in architectural history we should not ignore this fact but investigate it as significant not only of the nature of Victorian architecture but also of its new attraction for us. These ambiguities converged, or may be interpreted as converging, on one issue—that of style; and one might add to Humphry House's list of incompatible opposites which the Victorians were trying and failing to hold together the intense desire to have a style of their own while remaining convinced that style is a matter of ornament. Every Victorian building of any consequence is a statement of stylistic belief—either a belief in one style, or in the peaceful coexistence of styles (eclecticism), or in the efficacy of a mixed style. Nowhere is there any escaping this question of style and I doubt if we can fully respond to any major Victorian creation in architecture, not even the magisterial creations of Cockerell or Butterfield's noblest churches, without rekindling in our minds the style problem as it rankled and chafed in its creator's mind. Since an interest in choice of style is to us something totally unreal, an exercise of this kind is very difficult.

At this point I want to call evidence from the Victorian world itself, and I shall do so in the person of an architect of whom you may or may not have heard—Robert Kerr.[4] Kerr was born in 1823 and died in 1904. He built one fairly important city building and some country houses and wrote several books, but his significance for us now is that he was a man of acute intelligence and exceptional eloquence who was constantly being asked to address his professional colleagues on professional affairs and was fully reported whenever he did so. His speeches range over more than forty years and give us a remarkably vivid picture of the moods of the profession in the fifties, sixties, and seventies. We first meet him in 1846 as a young man of twenty-three, leading a group of discontented draftsmen and articled pupils in founding what was to become the Architectural Association. Kerr had recently crossed the Atlantic and, in his own words, "imbibed certain American notions," one of which seems to have been that English architectural ideas were due for a thorough spring-cleaning. Architecture he believed was a fine art and nothing else. It had nothing to do with archeology, old churches, drains, supervision of builders, or party-wall disputes; nothing to do with the Institute of British Architects and the Vitruvian fuddy-duddies who conducted it. Copyism, whether of Roman, Italian, or Gothic models, and the spirit of "precedent" were the great evils. The architect's imagination must be unfettered and as for style it was simply a question of creating for the nineteenth century a style appropriate to its new powers and new materials.[5] That was Kerr at twenty-three. Having as yet built nothing, the "new style" remained, for him, a shining new thing just around the corner.

Next, Kerr at thirty-seven. In 1860 he read, at the Architectural Exhibition, a paper called "The Battle of the Styles,"[6] a title appropriate to the year of Lord Palmerston's final rejection of Gilbert Scott's design for the Government Offices. Kerr is still more an observer than a participant, and the paper concludes with a valuable eyewitness account of the state of the battleground at that moment. He divides contemporary English practitioners into three schools. First, the *Eclectic,* meaning the elder architects, Fellows of the Institute, who wrought equally in copyist versions of Greco-Roman, Italian, Gothic, and Tudor. Second, the *Ecclesiological,* meaning those who stood somewhat outside the profession, who followed Pugin and dealt almost exclusively with Gothic churches and their appendages. And, third, a school or category which he called *Latitudinarian.* This, clearly, was the school which interested him personally, and I want to dwell a little on what he meant by this because it is perhaps here that we can begin to get a true view of the Victorian problem. Latitudinarianism had much to do with the attitudes of young men like Charles Gray, George Truefitt, and C. F. Hayward, who under Kerr's leadership had founded the Architectural Association in 1847. They had started out with a quest for the "modern" (incidentally, the first use of the expression "modernism" in relation to architecture which I know occurs in the title of a paper read at the A.A. in 1860)[7]—the new architecture of the new age of steam and iron. But the "modern" had turned out to be an illusion. Iron did, indeed, offer real, visible potentialities and was justified in the Crystal Palace. But Crystal Palace architecture, while undoubtedly suitable for a great exhibition, a palm house, or a railway shed, was suitable for little else. It did not solve the problem of style. Neither did the giant iron dome of the British Museum reading room; nor the bizarre equivalents of Gothic in the galleries of the Oxford Museum; nor the sheds of Paddington Station. In this quandary—the sheer inapplicability of the "modern" idea—the young men had turned to a new phenomenon altogether, the phenomenon of John Ruskin. And with Ruskin came, according to Kerr, latitudinarianism.

Now Ruskin in 1860 looked very different from the way he looks today. Still in early middle age he was known to architects almost exclusively through *The Seven Lamps of Architecture* (1849) and *The Stones of Venice* (1851 and 1853). In these he had written very movingly about Gothic architecture, but never for a moment had he proposed, recommended, or supported anything in the nature of a Gothic revival, or any revival. Not himself an architect, he skirted the whole question of what forms the modern architect should set down on his drawing board. A "new style," on the other hand, he thought a childish irrelevance. He had spoken on this subject at the Architectural Association in 1857: "If you are not content with a Palladio, you will not be content with a Paxton, and I pray you to get rid of the idea of there being any necessity for the invention of a new style."[8]

This sounds like a snub from a total reactionary, but in fact it was a release. Ruskin pointed to *no* style. His plates of careful profiles from Venice were offered as illustrations of principle, not as things to copy. He gave precepts but no models. Thus the architect was free—free from "modernism" as well as from eclecticism. In this awful freedom, doubt grew.

To Kerr, Ruskin was "a latitudinarian from first to last—the high priest of latitudinarians." To us, this may seem an odd way of describing Ruskin, and when Kerr goes on to compare him with John Bright, the radical free trader, the characterization may seem even odder. But latitudinarianism in Kerr's sense was indeed a sort of free trade. It was a flux of styles, sometimes with an Italian, sometimes with a modern French base. If Italian, it would be the quattrocento palace style with a strong bias toward Romanesque; if French, it might be something deriving from the new Louvre, or that provocatively sliced and surfaced manner, as if done in cheese, illustrated from time to time in the *Revue Générale de l'Architecture* of César Daly. Whichever base was taken there was liberty, liberty, liberty—liberty to introduce polychromy in brick and tile, naturalistic ornament, and caps and bases not at all unlike the illustrations in *Stones of Venice*. Kerr approved it because it had served, he thought, to extinguish "copyism." Its faults he discerned as too keen a quest for novelties and an overvaluation of the picturesque.

In isolating "latitudinarianism" as a school of Victorian architecture distinct from the eclectic and the ecclesiological, Kerr offered the historian a hint which has never properly been taken. But if we look at the architecture of the 1860s and 1870s in quantity and analyze it, we soon begin to see not only that a very high proportion of it has to be put in the "latitudinarian" sector but that this is precisely the sector where we find everything which today strikes us as most profoundly, most typically and, very often, most ludicrously Victorian. It was the architecture of hotels, of early apartment blocks, of many railway buildings, of suburban houses by the hundred, of countless city offices and warehouses; it was the architecture of men who never came to much recognition as artists but who were in fact, in the material sense, among the most effective practitioners of the time. A view of Victorian architecture which excludes or forgets the latitudinarians would be as lopsided as a view of Victorian religion which excluded or forgot the nonconformists and freethinkers. The analogy is rather close. Just as the multiplication of sectarian views bears witness to the underlying religious doubts of the Victorians, so the multiplication of stylistic attitudes represents the bedevilment of architectural conviction.

Kerr has no more to tell us about "latitudinarianism" and when we meet him again in 1869, his mood has greatly changed. He has now built his most important buildings[9] and tried "latitudinarianism" in practice. Clearly it has not worked. He is now forty-six and Professor of the Arts of Construction at King's College, London. His lecture of 1869 is on something called the "architecturesque" in which he is groping once more, rather ineffectively, for that philosopher's stone of so many Victorian architects, the ungraspable abstraction behind style. The lecture is not important, but it ends with a cry of frustration which is deeply significant of the moment:

If we architects are guilty of so much that is spurious in artistic principle, there must be for this effect a corresponding and equivalent cause. Is there not here and there, in matters besides architecture, and in perhaps, much more important matters, a good deal of more or less spurious sentiment? Do we not live in the very age of spurious sentiment? History, philosophy, law, politics, poetry—is there not but too much of spuriousness in every one of these? Faith, hope, even charity, are they not conventional to the core? And if we, as custodians of an art whose essential attribute it is to reflect the character of the time, reflect this character all too faithfully, what less than this and what else than this, could we be expected to do?[10]

The tone of this speech is very different from that of the constructive and optimistic "latitudinarian" speech of only nine years earlier and a whole world away from the gallant speeches which Kerr made when, twenty-two years earlier, he was busy founding the Architectural Association. Here, just at the very moment when England had achieved the most prodigious expansion in the whole of her history there was, in architecture, total disillusionment. Everything suddenly seemed to have failed. Eclecticism in Kerr's sense had faded away from sheer inanition; its expositors were old or dead. "Modernism" in terms of materials and function was stultified by the narrowness of its applicability. The Gothic Revival had spent itself in the church-building movement, now on the eve of decline. And out of latitudinarianism nothing had come except mixtures which never really mixed and bold departures which never arrived.

It was around 1870 that the first great revulsion against Victorian architecture began. It was expressed at first only by a few philosophical onlookers, but as the decade advanced it became evident that the profession was under a cloud. There were vicious and derisive articles in the press.[11] In 1869 the Government dispensed with the only able architect in its service, Pennethorne.[12] At South Kensington also, Henry Cole resolutely preferred military engineers.[13] In 1871 the attacks began on Street's designs for the Law Courts.[14] In 1874 Ruskin snubbed the Royal Institute of Britain's Architect and its president, Scott, by declining the Royal Gold Medal.[15] Inside the profession there was the worry expressed by Kerr that no direction so far taken was the right one and that honest building had come into the hands of the engineers. Kerr himself called architecture "the most unpopular profession of modern times."[16] He began to think that the only reasonable course for English architecture was to move closer to French classicism.[17] By 1891 he was dismissing Ruskin, hero of his "latitudinarian" phase, as a vaporer.[18] As for English architecture in general it had moved, by 1880, into a relaxed exploitation of all the Renaissance styles within reach: English, Flemish, Dutch, French, Italian, and Spanish. This new eclecticism caused no heart-burning, raised no fundamental issues and had its apotheosis in the *oeuvre* of Richard Norman Shaw. By 1900 Victorian architecture in its crucial phase was not only dead but had been buried for thirty years.

I have sketched a picture of early- and mid-Victorian architecture in terms of doubt and failure because I follow Humphry House in believing that in all the mass of evidence about the Victorians and their works these are among the essential clues to understanding and therefore have a strong bearing on our present-day evaluations. I want now to conclude with some observations on the kind of evaluations and evaluators who, since the nineteenth century closed, have brought us to where we stand today—the ground from which further studies must depart. We must start, I think, with our old friend, Robert Kerr and the extensive additions he contributed, when he was 68, to the 1891 edition of James Fergusson's *History of the Modern Styles of Architecture*. Based on forty years of personal observation and personal knowledge of many of the chief participants, it is good and precise in its account of the situation in 1851 but thereafter becomes more or less a catalogue of outstanding or characteristic works with conventional comments. Certainly at that time the Victorian period *was* too close to be critically observed and one can understand the despair which induced Sir Banister Fletcher, even as late as 1948, in his *History of Architecture on the Comparative Method* to deal with the whole of the English nineteenth century and the twentieth up to his own time by providing a "Who's Who" in two columns, one headed "Classical School," the other "Gothic School." A more misleading symmetry could hardly be imagined.

The first serious and comprehensive studies of Victorian architecture were those of Hermann Muthesius, the German architect, eventual founder of the Deutscher Werkbund, who was attached for seven years to the German embassy in London with a brief to report on the condition of English architecture.

His first book, on church-building, appeared in 1901.[19] It is not a history of Victorian church architecture but a critical review with a proper sense of historical connectedness. Scrupulously fair in his treatment of Pugin, Butterfield, and Street, Muthesius is yet very evidently a man of his time. The first church he really likes is Pearson's St. Peter's, Vauxhall; he admires Brooks for his appealing simplicity; but above all he loves J. D. Sedding, as Butterfield's true successor, a man of the Morris persuasion and "the apostle of a new era." Muthesius's three-volume work on the English house (1908–1910) shows the same approach.[20] He is not very interested in chronology; he is writing about what were, after all, still to him "modern times" and simply reviewing the recent architectural achievements of one country for consideration in another. But in doing so he is immensely erudite, serious, and solid.

Nothing as substantial as Muthesius was written about Victorian architecture between 1910 and the appearance of Henry-Russell Hitchcock's *Early Victorian Architecture*, from the Yale University Press, in 1954. Masterly as it is in comprehensiveness, accuracy of description, and the wisdom of its critical analyses, I still wonder if Hitchcock reaches down to the disturbing issues which underlie the whole Victorian performance—issues which, I admit, can hardly come very much to the surface in a survey whose terminal date is 1851.

Between Muthesius and Hitchcock what has been written? Three names immediately spring to mind: Goodhart-Rendel, Kenneth Clark, and, in a class entirely his own, John Betjeman. These are the names of three writers who, before 1938, did more than any others to redirect attention to Victorian architecture, though, oddly, they have produced among them no historical work much more substantial than an essay or set of essays.

H. S. Goodhart-Rendel, who died in 1959, was a most rare person.[21] Grandson and heir of the wealthy Lord Rendel, he became obsessed as a boy with a curiosity, most uncommon in an English patrician, about architects and the practice of architecture. He was a richly gifted musician, but an antipathy to the Germanic sententiousness in which his master, Donald Tovey, was involved induced him to leave music for architecture. In the First World War he was commissioned in a Guards regiment and there discovered that his real genius was, after all, for military command—he wrote a handbook to company drill. Returning reluctantly to architecture in 1922, he enjoyed a considerable practice and built churches, office buildings, and houses, none of which has been widely admired but none of which lacks originality and devoted care. He was president of the R.I.B.A. He wrote and lectured, mostly on and around the subject of Victorian architecture, and he compiled an almost complete card index of nineteenth-century British churches, giving their dates and architects, sometimes with critical comments of a highly personal kind.

Goodhart-Rendel was no art historian; indeed, he disliked art history. He was an architect—an architect who studied history not in the conventional manner of the textbooks, from antiquity to now, but *backwards*. He never had any formal training, but his effective masters were Sir Charles Nicholson, Beresford Pite, and Halsey Ricardo. Through these late Victorians he took great pains to know about and appreciate *their* masters, the mid-Victorians, and in the twenties and thirties he was the only man who really knew about them. He delivered his knowledge, or fragments of it, in one particular vehicle, the 6,000-word lecture. These lectures (some of which have been collected into books)[22] are, on the face of it, very slight things: entertainments—fastidious, epigrammatic entertainments. Nevertheless, they contain the remarkable insight of an architect who has in some perverse, egotistical way attached himself to this forgotten school to the extent that he can, by the most delicate indication of this or that peculiarity of a building, in a few words bring it freshly into the listener's mind and induce a new appreciation.

Goodhart-Rendel's influence on his younger contemporaries has been great, and Kenneth Clark's tribute to him is deserved: "The father of us all, whose kindness to his unworthy children is made more remarkable by the fact that he can see through all their pretences."

Kenneth Clark's own contribution to Victorian architectural studies is more easily described. It is contained in one book— *The Gothic Revival: An essay in the History of Taste*, published in 1928 and republished in 1950, by which time it had become, in its author's words, "a period piece." Here was a young man of twenty-five, exceedingly clever, fresh from Oxford and the tutelage of the omniscient C. F. Bell, taking what was then a dim theme, almost a black theme, and handling it with so much literary grace that it achieved an entertainment value somewhat on the level of Lytton Strachey's *Eminent Victorians* of ten years earlier. It had, to be sure, none of Strachey's destructive irony; it was a sympathetic investigation of its subject which, in its later chapters reopened forgotten careers (Pugin, Scott) and forgotten episodes (the building of the Oxford museum, the Government Offices competition) which were found more entertaining than could possibly have been expected. On the other hand, it is obvious that Kenneth Clark, on his way to more serious engagements with Berenson and Italian painting, had never brought himself to look very hard at Victorian buildings. He had only, in 1928, read one essay by Goodhart-Rendel. So his book is quite truly what he now calls it—a "period piece"—the work of one of the generation which was young in the twenties, looking back at the Victorians with a rather inhibited curiosity and reluctant to go too deeply into what they actually did. So problems of analysis are avoided (Butterfield earns only a few laconic references, Street fewer still), and the author sums up with the view that although the revival "could never produce agreeable architecture" its doctrine did have a permanent and beneficial effect in the acceptance of solid and conscientious building. This, as it happens, had been one of Muthesius's conclusions in 1901.

Clark's book certainly had the effect of making Victorian architecture a subject for further speculation. It was followed in 1930 by the work of another author—a *jeu d'esprit* called

Amphion, or the Nineteenth Century. The book has every appearance of being thrown off by a slightly supercilious amateur with an address in Chelsea, but it is actually the work of a bluff Yorkshire architect from Hull, Dudley Harbron. The writing is tiresomely flippant, but Harbron knew a lot, and this little work should not be overlooked.

But the man who, since 1928, has done more to resurrect and adorn the subject of Victorian architecture is, of course, John Betjeman. His story, though, is a mystery of our times and it may be that, as in some other things, we are too close to it to understand. Betjeman has not written even one book about Victorian architecture nor ever to my knowledge promoted any serious general claims for its qualities.[23] Yet his name has become an illuminant and a sanction; through him, kindliness toward Victorian architecture is permitted to thousands whose habits of mind would drive them in a quite other direction. How has this been done? The answer is, I suppose, to be found in his verses. These are never, or rarely, about Victorian architecture, but a great many of them draw upon childhood impressions of those layers and fragments of the Victorian world still embedded in the Edwardian world where Betjeman grew up. A child always sees the tantalizing *outside* of a great world which he will never enter because when he is grown up it will be dead. The inside remains a mystery and the shell between the two may be, as in some Betjeman poems, a sharp call to explore. But I doubt if even the circulation (which is wide) of Betjeman's poems can altogether account for the enormous influence he has had. A better answer may be simply the inflation of what was once a private joke, to which Betjeman's name got attached, into what one can only call the national humor. Back in the early thirties, observation and classification of Victoriana was, indeed, a joke, shared here and there. It was a game of recognition, and such games tend to be wildly infectious. Then came the war and the new literacy, county guides, Pevsner, television; and the little private joke of *Architectural Review* circles of the early thirties burst into the ocean in which, today, earnest scholarship, sheer silliness, poetic evocation, and crass nostalgia all go sailing.

Goodhart-Rendel, Clark, and Betjeman have been the main agents of the bringing back to notice of that lost world of English architecture which I characterized earlier as a failure. Would Rendel have agreed with that verdict? He would not, I think, have liked the question. He would insist on taking each building on its merits and judging it not as a historian but as an architect. Nevertheless, it was precisely the awkward aspects of Victorian things which excited his love of paradox, as who should say: "Look at this building you so much despise: look at this and this and see!—it is, after all, in its way, beautiful!"

Kenneth Clark, of course, was writing at a time when and in a cultural climate where the failure of Victorian architecture was accepted as proven, and he did not then challenge the prevailing opinion. Neither did Dudley Harbron. As for Betjeman I cannot help feeling that a failed period of architectural endeavor might have for him a special meaning, becoming a thing to like because it was so poignantly human as to have failed. I wonder if, for others besides Betjeman, this may not be a deep-seated, unacknowledged enticement.

But all this writing is past. Today, I doubt if Victorian resurrections can be exhibited as paradoxical or the subject any longer be allowed to be "amusing." The field is open to the deadpan historian, the serious student, and the scholar equipped not so much with charm and wit (those powerful deodorants so much in favor in the twenties and thirties) as with unlimited patience and real insight. I believe that any such students, adventuring into Victorian architecture, will have to ponder this problem of failure. There is no avoiding it, and I doubt if there is any point in trying to find a politer name. It was no mean failure; there was no weariness, no sense of inevitable decline. On the contrary, *never* in English architecture was there present more brilliant talent than between 1840 and 1870; never was there more powerful draftsmanship, more dedicated research, more painstaking inquiry; never was there such industry and application, never such seriousness, such energy. Is then "failure" the right word? Can it be that some critic, perhaps in the near future, having looked deeply into the whole of Victorian architecture—not merely at the church-building geniuses but all the lower schools, the latitudinarians in all their diversities—will discover some standpoint from which the whole thing looks right after all and an Act of Settlement becomes possible? I cannot think so because any such discovery would at once be exposed as a fraud by the documented self-criticism of the age itself. I believe that in the architecture of the Victorians we are faced with a unique and huge distortion of social and artistic relationships; and it may well be in that distortion and the penetration of its effects into the buildings of the time and, indeed far beyond, that its fascination for the modern mind lies.

II. Two Victorian Stations

THE VICTORIAN AGE introduced railways and along with railways, railway stations and railway hotels, buildings which offer themselves as conspicuous material for the investigation of what Victorian architecture is. For this inquiry I have chosen two famous London examples, King's Cross and St. Pancras, the latter with its hotel. I have chosen these partly for their intrinsic historical interest and partly because both buildings are under threat. Both are listed for protection under the Town and Country Planning Acts, but in the last resort neither will survive unless an appropriate use can be found for them. At the moment it seems that we can be fairly optimistic about St. Pancras Hotel becoming again a hotel; of St. Pancras shed the fate is doubtful and the prospects for King's Cross are not bright.

King's Cross was the fifth London terminal to be built, and we cannot fairly evaluate it as a building without observing how it stands in relation to its predecessors. The first London terminal was at Euston Square for the London and Birmingham Railway, built between 1835 and 1840 on a plan by Robert Stephenson with platforms, sheds, and permanent way by Charles Fox.[1] It was not a terminal in the full sense but rather a reception base where passengers boarded coaches which were then hauled on an endless cable to the locomotive depot at Chalk Farm. This reception base was prefaced and axially connected with

1. Euston Station,
London: portico and
lodges, 1835-1840.

the map of London by a monumental portico with flanking
lodges, designed by Philip Hardwick (Fig. 1). Fox's iron roofs
and columns were adaptations of familiar industrial types of the
period, but Hardwick's portico was only a monster version of
the kind of thing which noblemen were accustomed to build
at the entrances to their parks. It was the entrance, as it were,
to the railway company's estate. The problem of a railway station as an architectural subject was not brought into focus.

The next London terminus was built in 1837–1838 at Nine
Elms for the London and Southampton Railway as part of the
first installment of its line from Battersea to Woking[2] (Fig 2).
The company's architect was William Tite, then thirty-nine and
not yet the declared winner of the Royal Exchange competition.
Tite built in front of the platforms an office building consisting
of five open arches between rusticated end pavilions, a familiar
Neoclassical arrangement close in style to Fowler's Hungerford
Market completed four years earlier and very evidently a product of the Durand school of functional classicism.

Next came the station of the London and Greenwich railway at London Bridge[3] (Fig. 3). This railway had been content
since 1836 with wooden platforms behind an iron gate. But

2. Nine Elms Station, London, 1837-1888 (*British Rail*).

3. London Bridge Station, 1844 (*R.I.B.A. Library*).

4. Bricklayers Arms Station, London, 1844 (*Illustrated London News*).

TWO VICTORIAN STATIONS

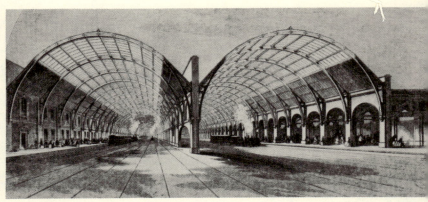

5. King's Cross
Station, London,
1851-1852: section
through the sheds
(*The Builder, 1851*).

after making arrangements for the London and Croydon, the
London and Brighton, and the South Eastern to run into the
station, the railway doubled the number of tracks and in 1844
built, jointly with the Brighton company, a new station building. The executant architect for both was Henry Roberts, whose
Fishmongers' Hall on the far side of London Bridge was just
ten years old, although the facade buildings are said to have
been by the resident architect, Thomas Turner. Whoever really
designed it, the station exhibited another solution of the station
problem—this time an Italian villa, not unlike the Italian villa
which Charles Barry had lately completed for Lord Tankerville
at Walton-on-Thames.[4] Raised on ground that was made up to
the level of the viaduct which carried the line to Greenwich, the
station with its tower and belvedere must have made a pretty
picture. In 1845 the Greenwich surrendered itself on lease to
the South Eastern and the Brighton amalgamated with the Croydon to become the London Brighton and S. Coast Railway. In
1850 the two resulting companies reconstructed the whole station.

But before these changes, the rivalries at London Bridge

TWO VICTORIAN
STATIONS

22

had produced yet another terminus. Shortly before the building
of the Roberts-Turner station in 1844 the South Eastern and the
Croydon, as a protest against what they considered excessive
tolls charged by the Greenwich for the use of its lines, obtained
powers to build their own station off the Old Kent Road at
Bricklayers Arms[5] (Fig. 4). The station was completed in 1844.
The architect was Lewis Cubitt, younger brother of the great
builder and, as we shall shortly see, architect of King's Cross.
Cubitt was born in 1799, and so was four years younger than

TWO VICTORIAN
STATIONS

23

8. King's Cross
Station, London, 1968
(*photo: Timothy
Summerson*).

Sir Charles Barry, a year older than Decimus Burton, three years older than Pennethorne. His earlier works, from 1824, were done for the Cubitt firm and no doubt include their distinguished Greek-detailed blocks of houses in the Gordon Square area and in Belgravia. By 1837, however, he had switched to the coarse and mannered Italian of his Lowndes Square houses.[6] This was *not* the sophisticated, finely modeled Italian of Barry but something allied to the much more cranky villa style of Charles Parker's *Villa Rustica* and J. C. Loudon's *Encyclopedia of Cottage, Farm and Villa Architecture,* both of 1832. The style was supposedly based on Italian vernacular. It was remotely related via Papworth and Thompson to Nash's villas of around 1800. Its expositors claimed for it the merits of convenience, variety, and character. Arrangements impossible in the conventional styles were allowed in this and if convenience suggested some very bizarre arrangements they could, with proper judgment, be induced to convey character. The philosophy of the style, though in a Tudor context, is well explained by Edward Buckton Lamb in the preface to his *Studies of Ancient Domestic*

Architecture of 1846 (to which I shall make further reference).

The style grew from the impulses of fashion reacting against the smooth, flat, residue of Greek revivalism. Its vaunted adaptability to "convenience" made it a natural medium for new problems, such as railway architecture, and Lewis Cubitt used it at Bricklayers Arms with vigor and originality. The station sheds were on the Euston model, but less successful—they collapsed shortly after being built. The facade expressed in a quite new way the function of the whole. "In" and "out" arches at each end marked the arrival and departure courts. Three arches in the center gave immediate access to the railhead, perhaps for ceremonial occasions or the introduction of heavy equipment, while between the sets of arches were triple doorways under heavy bracketed hoods giving access to the booking offices on one side and the parcels office on the other. The center of the composition broke out and up on a vertical slab emphatically exhibiting a clock and surmounted by a bell turret—a happy expression of the intimate association of time with successful railway enterprise. The bracketed hoods and the bell turrets derive directly from plates in *Villa Rustica*, the style of that work being further accentuated by Italian pantiles along the top of the screen wall and on the hoods and bell turret. Bricklayers Arms was a spirited venture, the very opposite of the lordly and conservative Euston portico, which only acquired an emotional railway association when somebody thought of calling it "the gateway to the north." The idea of a functionally expressive screen spread across the ends of a set of railway sheds was the theme of Lewis Cubitt's next enterprise, King's Cross.

The Great Northern Railway had a temporary station at Maiden Lane in 1850 but in 1851 obtained powers to build a new station at King's Cross on the site of an old smallpox hospital.[7] In principle, we have the same arrangement as at Bricklayers Arms—a screen placed across the open ends of twin railway sheds. Here, however, the sheds have grown into important engineering structures. Nothing as ambitious had been attempted. On a small scale the Eastern Counties first terminus

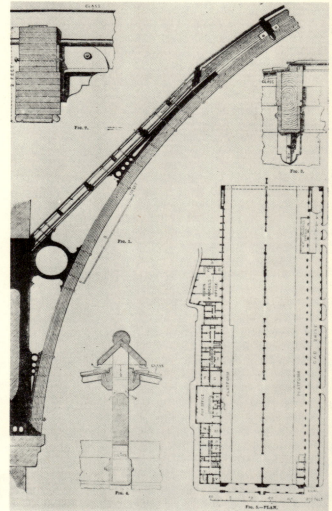

9. King's Cross
Station, London,
1851-1852: details of
iron and bent timber
roof rib and plan of
station (*The Builder*,
1852).

TWO VICTORIAN
STATIONS

26

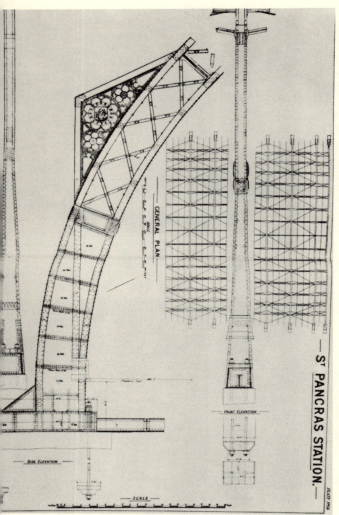

10. St. Pancras
Station, London,
1863-1867: details of
iron roof rib (A. T.
Walmisley, *Iron
Roofs*, 1884).

TWO VICTORIAN
STATIONS

11. St. Pancras
Station, London,
1863-1867: the open
(north) end of the
shed (A. T.
Walmisley, *Iron
Roofs*, 1884).

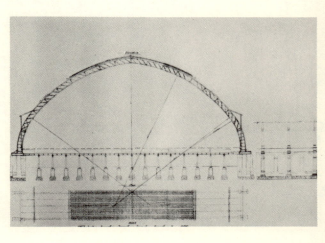

12. St. Pancras
Station, London,
1863-1867: section
through shed (A. T.
Walmisley, *Iron
Roofs*, 1884).

TWO VICTORIAN
STATIONS

28

at Shoreditch (later called Bishopsgate) seems to have had arched
roofs with circular ventilating apertures, and in the north John
Dobson's Central Station at Newcastle (opened 1850) was like
a Euston increased in all dimensions with the trusses boldly
arched and carrying a ventilating "clerestory."[8] But King's Cross
has semicircular roofs 280 feet long thrown across a span of
105 feet from the outer walls of the station to a line of brick
piers and arches down the center (Fig. 5).

Stylistically, Lewis Cubitt shifted his ground from the cranky
picturesque Italian of Bricklayers Arms and *Villa Rustica* to something more serious and monumental (Fig. 6). King's Cross has
its source in the philosophy and example of J. N. L. Durand, the
author of the *Précis des Lecons* first published in 1802 but republished with further material in 1813 and 1820. Durand, who
taught at the Ecole Polytechnique, had a certain contempt for

both Vitruvius and Laugier, despised ornament as a frivolous extra, and believed architecture to be an affair of economics and construction organized in a methodical way. He admitted, however, a certain limited reliance on ancient Rome. As Kaufmann[9] observes, he was just the man for the nineteenth century, especially one might add, the English nineteenth century—though in fact his influence is seen more strongly in Germany, where his book was published in translation in 1831. In England Durand's ideas are reflected in the markets of Charles Fowler, notably the Hungerford Market of 1831–1833 and the Lower Market at Exeter built about 1835. Durand's influence is also reflected, as we have seen, in the Nine Elms station and in the monumental design (possibly by Brunel) for the building for the Great Exhibition of 1851, superseded at the last moment by Paxton's Crystal Palace.[10] In the exactly contemporary design of King's Cross it is unambiguous (Figs. 6 and 7).

In the layout of the station there was the same duality of arrival and departure as at Bricklayers Arms. The station was divided into two by a long spine of brick arches. From these sprang the two great roofs carried on semicircular ribs. In the first instance these ribs were of laminated timber, not laminated trusses of the kind invented by Philibert de l'Orme but trusses consisting of sixteen 1½″ deals bolted together in a curve (Fig. 9). This was a fairly recent French innovation (Col. Emy of the Génie Militaire, 1819). Fowler had used it at Exeter (the Lower Market), and Paxton was using it at the Crystal Palace.[11] At King's Cross the timber became defective owing to the effects of smoke and was replaced by iron in 1869, the iron being fitted into the original cast-iron shoes.[12]

The station sheds at King's Cross are self-standing on the lateral and center walls, the end wall being merely a massive screen. In the design as published in the *Builder* for 1851 (Fig. 6) we can see that Cubitt was thinking in the sort of Roman Bath terms appropriate to a discipline of Durand[13]—round arches under open pediments—but in execution the parapet was made level. The two great seven-ring arches abut against a center and

14. G. Gilbert Scott: St. Pancras Hotel, London, c. 1865 (*R. I. B. A. Library*).

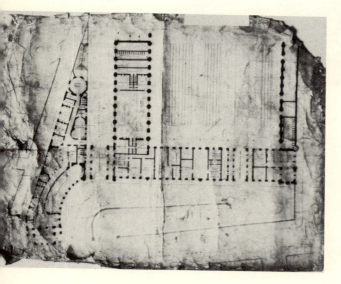

15. G. Gilbert Scott: St. Pancras Hotel, London, ground floor plan, c. 1865 (*R. I. B.A. Library*).

TWO VICTORIAN STATIONS

31

16. (above) St. Pancras Hotel, London, entrance tower, 1865-1871 (*National Monuments Record*).

17. (at right) G. Gilbert Scott: St. Pancras Hotel, study for entrance tower, 1865 (*R. I. B. A. Library*).

two lateral pylons, the center pylon carrying a clock turret, the only feature betraying Cubitt's taste for the Italianate (Fig. 8). Within each of the arches stand sets of three segmental arches, now totally obscured from view, forming an entrance loggia or continuous porch. To left and right of this very striking front are two extensions. That on the left (departure) is the end of a long block containing booking halls, waiting rooms, etc. That on the right (arrival) has a rusticated arch, all in brick, leading to a drive-in for cabs. These two adjuncts are not too well integrated and are often overlooked.

18. (at left) St. Pancras Hotel, London, 1865-1871 (*photo: Timothy Summerson*).

19. (above) G. Gilbert Scott: St. Pancras Hotel, study for hotel entrance front, c. 1865 (*R.I.B.A. Library*).

Nobody, I think, could call King's Cross a wholly successful composition, but its twin arches are immensely impressive in themselves, and the emphatic duality, so clearly symbolic of arrival and departure, is a fine piece of dramatic realism. The clock turret is hardly a success. It looks as if it had been put there like a mantelpiece clock and could at any moment be replaced by a bust of Prince Albert; one wonders why Cubitt did not continue his center pylon vertically without a break, as at Bricklayers Arms. Some contemporary critics dismissed King's Cross as hopelessly mean, but others approved. The *Builder* of

TWO VICTORIAN STATIONS

20. The Cloth Hall,
Ypres (J. Fergusson,
*Handbook of
Architecture,* 1855).

21. Town Hall,
Preston, Lancs., 1862-
1867 (*The Builder,*
1862).

22. Kelham Hall,
Notts., 1858-1862
(*photo: M. W.
Barley*).

TWO VICTORIAN
STATIONS

1851 put its merits succinctly; the architect, it said, has depended "wholly for effect on the largeness of some of the features, the fitness of the structure for its purpose, and a characteristic expression of that purpose." This may seem to us pretty just. Fergusson, writing ten years after the station was built (1862), found that it "has the merit of being entirely truthful," the clock tower being "a perfectly legitimate feature." "The one great defect," however, in Fergusson's view, was that "the style is so simple and grand that it ought to have been executed in granite, while it is carried out in simple brick."[14] Fergusson thought brick demanded a lighter treatment with shallower arches (consonant with the lightness of the roof structure) and makes reference to the light and ornate treatment of brick in Schinkel's *Bauschule* in Berlin. Money could have been saved, he says, on sheer mass of brick and used for ornament, thus making the building more properly architecture. This is a curious point of view to us who probably enjoy the sheer *mass* of the pylons and *depth* of the arches more in their brick nature than if they

23. Beckett's Bank, Leeds, Yorks., 1864–1866 (*National Monuments Record*).

TWO VICTORIAN STATIONS

were in granite. The kind and degree of emotional involvement with brick is a variable in nineteenth-century architectural history which is hard to grasp. It is interesting, though, that King's Cross always had its champions. Ten years later again, after Fergusson, in 1872, comes J. T. Emmett writing in the *Quarterly Review:* "The Great Northern Terminus is not graceful, but it is simple, characteristic, and true. No one would mistake its nature and use."[15] Admittedly this cautious praise was incidental to a tremendous attack on the vulgarity of St. Pancras Hotel. In fact, the use of King's Cross as a stick to beat St. Pancras with has been a common exercise up to our own day. But on all grounds King's Cross has held its own pretty well.

24. G. Gilbert Scott: St. Pancras Hotel, design for dining room, c. 1866 (*R. I. B. A. Library*).

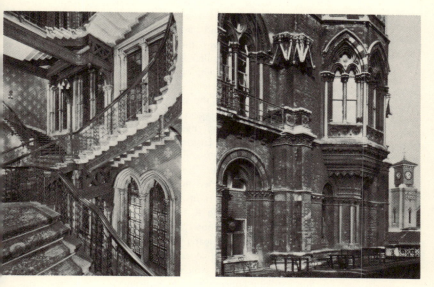

25. (at left) St. Pancras Hotel, London, 1865-1871: staircase at first floor landing (*National Monuments Record*).

26. (above) St. Pancras Hotel, London, 1865-1871: detail of oriel window on clock tower (*National Monuments Record*).

TWO VICTORIAN STATIONS

37

As we leave King's Cross there is one important point to be made. Architect and engineer here were one and the same person; the engineering is of the empirical kind in which accumulated experience and judgment by eye still counted more than calculation. King's Cross was almost the last instance of such a situation. When Paddington Station was built in 1852–1854 a marriage between engineering and architecture was attempted.[16] Brunel designed the station sheds but called in Matthew Digby Wyatt as a sort of artistic consultant, the expressed object of the collaboration being to avoid any recurrence to existing styles, and "make the experiment of designing everything in accordance with the structural purpose, or natures of the materials employed

—iron and cement."[17] This is a different philosophy from that of the Durand school, since it deliberately excludes reliance on Rome. The design problem is left in mid-air, the result being, in the case of Paddington, a curious fluttering in and out of Gothic, *quattrocento,* and Oriental motifs with no real integration. The experiment was interesting and sincere but was not repeated, though its results are echoed in innumerable provincial stations. After Paddington, the divorce between architect and engineer was complete. It was ratified in the consciences of railway directors by the practice, begun at Paddington, of planting a huge, ornate, and profitable hotel designed by an architect in front of the sheds designed by engineers. Hotels had sprung up earlier. Euston got its two hotels, flanking the portico, as early as 1839–1840. Nine Elms had a hotel, and at King's Cross Cubitt built a hotel after he had built the station. But none of these affected the view of the station or had the monumentality of P. C. Hardwick's Great Western Hotel—a sort of French *hotel de ville* with the addition of quasi-Jacobean towers with "Hatfield" roofs, completely hiding the station.

After Paddington nearly all London terminals consist of crude engineering sheds concealed behind lavishly architectural hotels—hotels of a type which somebody characterized as "one of those striking conceptions which distinctively mark the civilization of the age."[18] To Victoria in 1860–1861 came the colossal Grosvenor, by J. T. Knowles; between 1864 and 1866 Charing Cross and Cannon Street arrived—Hawkshaw's engineering at the back, E. M. Barry's architecture in front in both cases.[19] Then came St. Pancras. At St. Pancras we see two things. In the shed, the highest flight in Victorian engineering in this particular field. In the hotel, the most emphatic and uncompromising application of Gothic revivalism to a secular purpose.

The Midland Railway in 1860 was a flourishing regional organization, weakly linked to London by a system of "running powers" on other companies' lines.[20] The system was never entirely satisfactory and in the Exhibition year of 1862 broke down altogether, thus precipitating a decision by the Midland directors to construct their own line from Bedford to London and to buy property on which to build their own London terminus. Powers were obtained in 1863, a property was bought on advantageous terms, nicely sited between the existing termini at Euston and King's Cross and the company instructed their engineer, W. H. Barlow, to prepare plans.

From this point the building of the shed at St. Pancras proceeded with what, in retrospect, seems a remorseless logic. Here was an example of the new complexity which was invading nineteenth-century building—a complexity made up of social, economic, and technological factors overwhelming the simple traditional equation of material and disposition. At St. Pancras these factors were brought into harmony with remarkable success. First, the level of the line on arrival at St. Pancras was dictated by the necessary clearance of the Regents Canal. This meant that the platform level in the station would be from 12 to 15 feet above the gently sloping Euston Road. Thus the platforms would have space under them to be supported on vaults. These vaults would have economic value as storage space. They could be made of brick arches—as they were, for instance, at Charing Cross. But it was seen that there would be a greater yield of storage space if, instead of massive brick piers, there were iron stanchions. Furthermore, it was seen that the principal takers of this storage space would be the brewers of Burton-on-Trent. These brewers had their own traditional methods of barrel storage, methods dictating a unit of 29 feet 4 inches. This dimension was therefore adopted as a module for the entire area.

Then came the question of covering. The most obvious procedure was to cover the whole area in two relatively easy spans of around 120 feet—a little more than King's Cross. But an objection to this was that the central line of columns between the two spans would have to penetrate below the platforms to massive bases which would not only disrupt the grid of the storage space but stand dangerously over the St. Pancras branch of the new underground railway. Also, the general manager made a strong plea for a single span as favorable to flexibility of arrangement and rearrangement in as yet unforeseen circumstances. The company therefore directed Barlow to design a roof in a single span—the as yet unheard-of span of 240 feet. This he achieved with a roof consisting of pairs of iron lattice ribs making a section like a four-centered arch (there are actually six centers)—a Gothic shape but not for Gothic reasons: the shape was adopted as the best for resisting lateral wind pressures (Figs. 10 and 12). Now these ribs required either very secure anchorage at their bases or ties from foot to foot in each pair of ribs, or, preferably, both. They got both because Barlow not merely bolted them to granite and brick piers but used the continuous lines of joists which support the platforms over the vaults as ties connecting the feet of the ribs—ties which, being below the platforms, are conveniently unaffected by changes in temperature. Altogether, a beautifully clean and neat solution, giving a visually impressive, uncomplicated result.[21] (Figs. 11 and 13).

The actual curve of the roof was an optimum arrived at after calculation of the pressures generated by the dead load, snow, and wind. Insofar as temperature changes affect the roof, the result is only a slight rise or fall at the crown. The roof was made by the Butterley Iron Company and remains today in magnificent condition. Its span was not exceeded till the far less elegant roof of the Pennsylvania Station of Jersey City (252 feet) was built in 1888.[22]

With the station in building, the directors of the Midland turned their attention to plans for a hotel and in 1865 invited eleven well-known architects to submit drawings in competition. E. M. Barry was one of them—an obvious choice in view of his success at Charing Cross and Cannon Street. The others included George Somers Clarke, F. P. Cockerell, Alfred Darbishire (Baroness Burdett-Coutts's architect), Owen Jones, Lockwood and Mawson (of Bradford), and George Gilbert Scott. Scott declined more than once and competed only under strong pressure from one of the directors. He was awarded the first premium; G. Somers Clarke came next, then E. M. Barry. I have not found any of the designs of Scott's rivals. One would particularly like to see that of Owen Jones, the only competitor to have sufficient respect for Barlow's station to allow it prominence in his design.[23]

Scott, at this time, was fifty-four and had just completed his design for the Albert Memorial. He took a very cavalier attitude toward the conditions laid down by the Midland board. They asked for 150 bedrooms; he gave them 250 and accompanied his design by a thumping estimate of £316,000 (about £150,000 more than most of his rivals). There was a mild remonstrance from Somers Clarke on behalf of the other competitors.[24] One cannot help suspecting that Scott had been assured by his persuasive director friend that he was on a very good wicket.

He worked out the whole design in the course of a holiday at a small seaside hotel at Hayling in September and October, 1865. He tells us in the *Recollections* that "it was in the same style which I had almost originated several years earlier, for the government offices [in Whitehall—the date was 1856]." Palmerston, as everybody knows, had vetoed the design. Scott goes on: "I was glad to be able to erect one building in that style in London. I had carried it out already in a few instances, in the provinces; of which the most remarkable are the Town Hall at Preston, Kelham Hall in Nottinghamshire, and the Old Bank at Leeds."[25]

Now, this style. Note that Scott, who was never a man to underestimate his achievements, says that he *almost* originated the style. Is this a generous recognition that the Middle Ages rendered some slight assistance, or was he actually conscious that much in the Whitehall design was inspired by the design of 1855 for Deane and Woodward's Museum at Oxford? Maybe. In any case, the style as developed for the Whitehall competition of 1856 (Figs. 54 and 55) is certainly well on the way to St. Pancras.[26] The intermediate examples—Kelham Hall (1858–1862; Fig. 22), the Town Hall at Preston (1862–1867; Fig. 21) and Beckett's, now the Westminster, Bank, Leeds (1864–1866; Fig. 23) —do not seem to carry the style much further forward. Essentially it is based on north Italian, nonlinear, Gothic which allows for an even disposition of windows in an unbuttressed wall surface without looking like Batty Langley. These early French and English Gothic details are blended in to give character and richness to the whole. It is impossible not to admire the way it is done (Figs. 14–19). Never mind whether style-mixing is or is not proper architecture; the fact is that it is extremely difficult to do. It can only be done after years of dedication to eclectic studies and with a developed sensibility as to what will go with what. This is not copybook stuff; it is improvisation direct onto the drawing board. To fail to appreciate this is to fail hopelessly to understand Victorian architecture.

Scott tells us that at St. Pancras he "divested [his style] of the Italian element."[27] This is, on the face of it, not true and I think he must have meant simply that by the use of much shafting, tracery, canopies, and pinnacles he tried to give the design a more linear and northern look. There are certain obvious northern influences—the Cloth Hall at Ypres (Fig. 20) for the tower over the station entrance (Figs. 16 and 17) and some Dutch or Flemish town hall, Oudenarde perhaps, for the Euston Road gable with its huge pinnacles. The clock tower is one of Scott's many versions of the "Big Ben" idea. The bay design throughout is a fascinating combination of north Italian and English detail; on the first floor (Fig. 26) one catches a whiff of Bishop Bridport's tomb at Salisbury where Scott was conducting the restoration.

The plan of St. Pancras Hotel (Fig. 15) is original and ingenious. The main block is set back from the road to allow a generous and well-contrived ramped approach with a parallel ramped return. Then the west wing rushes forward in a curve to meet the highly ornate hotel entrance front to Euston Road (Figs. 18 and 19). Unfortunately there was not really room for so ambitious an exercise, an exercise Neoclassical rather than Gothic in spirit. The curve is not a quadrant but only a shallow segment, starting away gauchely from the tower. The entrance front on Euston Road is tremendously imposing when seen dead-on but painfully pretentious when it is discovered that after two bays along Midland Road, the side wall goes slipping away at an apologetic angle (Fig. 18).

The St. Pancras Hotel has always been the subject of ferocious criticism, never more so than when it was just finishing in 1872. When Scott refers to "one of the revilers of my profession" as having spoken of it "with abject contempt" he must, I think, mean J. T. Emmett—an architect himself and a good one—whose comments on King's Cross I have already quoted. In the same article in the *Quarterly Review* Emmett delivered himself as follows:

The . . . front [of the Hotel] is inconsistent in style, and meretricious in detail; a piece of common 'art manufacture' that makes the Great Northern front [King's Cross] appear by contrast positively charming. There is no relief or quiet in any part of the work. The eye is constantly troubled and tormented, and the mechanical patterns follow one another with such rapidity and perseverance, that the mind becomes irritated where it ought to be gratified and goaded to criticism where it should be led calmly to approve. There is here a complete travesty of noble associations, and not the slightest care to save these from sordid contact. An elaboration that might be suitable for a chapterhouse, or a Cathedral choir, is used as an 'advertising medium' for bagmen's bedrooms and the costly discomforts of a terminus hotel, and the architect is thus a mere expensive rival of the Company's head cook in catering for the low enjoyments of the great travelling crowd. . . . Here the public taste has been exactly suited, and every kind of architectural decoration has been made thoroughly common and unclean.[28]

Emmett adds that this kind of thing is the result of competitions among architects for the approval of judges whom they know to be incompetent.

There is perhaps some personal animus in Emmett's remarks, but there is also a good deal of justice. I think that Scott's often quoted remark that in his belief the building was "possibly *too good* for its purpose"[29] was an avowal that ornaments derived from cathedrals and shrines should be distributed with a little more reverence and discretion than he had exercised in this instance.

Yet are Emmett's criticisms in the long run justified? We can no longer feel his animosity against commercial travelers and what he calls "the low enjoyments of the great travelling crowd." All are long since dead and their vulgarity forgiven. We may understand Emmett's distaste (and Scott's implied guilt) for cathedral and chapter-house architecture being brought into a context which he considered low, but I doubt if we can really *feel* with him on this point. The building comes down to us as a lonely, obsolete monument, liberated from the emotional strife of its period. We can only judge it now, surely, in relation to our experience of what went before and what came after in English architecture, and how St. Pancras evolved from the given program. On the evidence, it seems that we have here a rather hasty improvisation in which the architect's thought has been dominated by the desire to expound a style which he believed he had invented. If we are to find St. Pancras Hotel interesting, it is necessary above all to find Scott's style interesting (I confess I do). And if we do find it interesting, we must in the last resort make our own intuitive judgments as to whether in the profiles, proportions, and modeling this interesting style gives the deeper satisfaction of an exceptional sensibility (my judgment is that it does not). That the building is too big for its site, that the skyline is chaotic and unreadable, and that the towers lack the prominence which their nature demands are, I think, points which few would dispute. But it is difficult to condemn the building wholly on these grounds; it always pleads for a second judgment and always on this special ground of style—the special ground of this Victorian generation and the quicksand, as I suggested in my first lecture, in which its reputation sank.

Internally, as you may imagine, St. Pancras Hotel is mostly bedrooms (now used as offices), but there were two grand features. One, which does not survive, was the long curved dining room (Fig. 24). The one which does is the spectacular "imperial" staircase (Fig. 25), on a plan of Baroque provenance, built of stone like an ordinary "geometrical" or cantilever stair but then strapped up for safety in a quantity of ironwork all of which is given a Gothic touch. Above is an admirably designed and constructed Gothic vault.

Now, having looked closely at King's Cross and St. Pancras and glanced at some earlier and contemporary stations, what have we found to assist us with our problem of evaluation? I would suggest that to most of us King's Cross suggests an acceptable union—a reasonable integration of architecture and engineering. It seems to have been so accepted in its time. It is a weak design in some ways by its own standards, which are standards left over from an earlier period, standards, however, acceptable over a wide area of European time. St. Pancras is a very different matter. Here we have, in effect, two disintegrations. First, the disintegration of architecture and engineering: the total separation of functional and "artistic" criteria, in separate heads and hands. Second, the disintegration of architecture itself by the compulsive obtrusion of the question of style.

The first disintegration is manifest in the essentially non-artistic design of the St. Pancras roof. Here we have rib shapes arrived at not by eye but by the application and combination of a series of calculations; their section and the distribution of rivets likewise based on the sole criterion of performance. Fergusson[30] felt the St. Pancras roof to be non-architecture and inhumanely too big; he would have preferred a double span.

The second disintegration is the one I am chiefly concerned with in this book. St. Pancras Hotel could be exhibited as representing the ultimate absurdity of the English situation around 1870: its distorted Neoclassical plan and oversized bulk hopefully modeled up into a picturesque architectural episode; the almost comic situation reached when the convertibility of Gothic to practical uses is too far tested. If St. Pancras Hotel were to be taken as fully and completely representative of English architecture in its time, the whole subject could be reduced to something small, sad, and interesting only for the extreme curiosity of the style problem. But it was not. Victorian architecture is nothing if not varied, and in the next two chapters I shall bring together other talents and other attitudes which present other and perhaps more difficult problems of evaluation.

III. Two London Churches

NO BUILDINGS of the Victorians offer themselves more conspicuously as subjects for criticism than their churches. The problems of evaluation may be brought into focus by a scrutiny of two London churches of the early sixties: St. James the Less, Thorndike Street (formerly Garden Street) off the Vauxhall Bridge Road; and St. Martin's, Vicar's Road, Gospel Oak. St. James's was built in 1858–1861, the architect being George Edmund Street. St. Martin's was built in 1862–1865, the architect being Edward Buckton Lamb. What these two churches have in common is that both were built by rich patrons and built in melancholy, poverty-stricken tracts of the London fringe as acts of Christian charity. That is to say, they have no tincture of the conventional London estate church, initiated by a developer and helped along toward a tower and spire by local subscriptions and grants from episcopal and other funds. Both St. James's and St. Martin's were built with ample means, sincere goodwill, and strong views as to churchmanship. In everything else they are different, and that is what makes the comparison instructive. I propose first to discuss the patrons of the two churches, then the architects, and finally the fabrics themselves. One important difference between the two churches, in the final outcome, is this. One, St. James's, was applauded as a fine and original work of art; its architect proceeded to become a national figure and

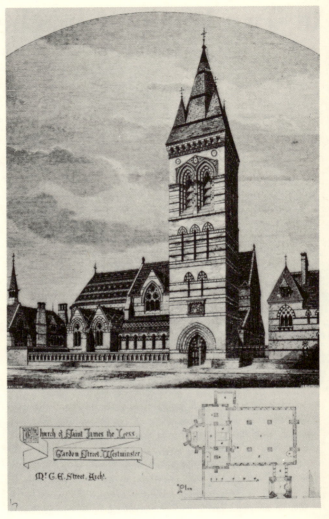

27. St. James-the-Less, Westminster, 1858-1861 (*The Builder*, 1861).

Church of Saint James the Less

Garden Street, Westminster

Mr G. E. Street, Arch't.

Plan

TWO LONDON
CHURCHES

48

CHURCH, HAVERSTOCK HILL.——Mr. E. B. Lamb, Architect.

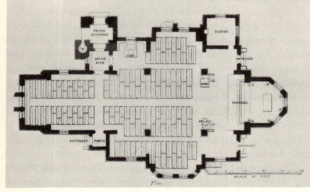

28. St. Martin, Gospel
Oak, London, 1862-
1865 (*The Builder*,
1866).

TWO LONDON
CHURCHES

49

29. Church group,
Boyne Hill,
Maidenhead, 1854-
1865 (*The Builder*,
1860).

one of the representative architects of his time. The other, St. Martin's, though praised by some, was either abused or ignored by most; its architect, though sufficiently successful, did not achieve fame and is only cursorily mentioned if at all in the reference books. The question in our minds is likely to be why, to sophisticated Victorians, one church was "good" and the other "bad." The answers, if they can be found, should be an instructive commentary on the Victorian mind and on the question of evaluation.

The founders of St. James the Less were three sisters, Misses Jane Emily, Mary Mostyn, and Penelope Anna Monk, born in

1823, 1826, and 1828 respectively. They were daughters of the Right Reverend James Henry Monk, Bishop of Gloucester and Bristol, formerly a Canon of Westminster, who died in 1856.[1] I can tell you nothing about them, though there must still be those who remember them for they died within a few months of each other, aged ninety-four, ninety-one, and eighty-nine in 1917. They lived in a magnificent house in Cadogan Square, designed for them by Street in 1879; it still stands, though altered, I believe, internally. The Monk family was well connected, and the sisters must have inherited considerable wealth. Their father, the Bishop, to whom the daughters' church is a memorial, was a notable scholar and a high churchman as things went in his time. His daughters followed him in that direction.

The builder of St. Martin's, Gospel Oak, was John Derby Allcroft, born at Worcester, apparently of middle-class parents in 1822. He became a manufacturer of gloves and head of the firm of Messrs. Dent, Allcroft and Company, London, and his wealth accrued through the spread of the fashion for wearing gloves from the upper classes through a large section of the female population. In 1864, at forty-two and just before the completion of St. Martin's, he married the daughter of a Hampshire gentleman. Allcroft was a businessman of austere and regular habits. Living in Lancaster Gate he walked every day to and from his office in the city. He had two sons and tradition has it that when he saw that they had no business ability he sent them to Harrow and set them up as country gentlemen.[2] He entered Parliament as a Conservative at the age of fifty-six in 1878 as one of the members for Worcester, having contested the seat unsuccessfully four years earlier.[3] By 1880 he had acquired the estate of Stokesay Castle, Shropshire, with its wonderful medieval house; and there, shortly before his death, he built the great Jacobean-style mansion called Stokesay Court designed for him by Thomas ("Victorian") Harris. According to his epitaph (in St. Martin's) "he was a great philanthropist and a leader in every work of charity and mercy and devoted his time fortune and energy to the relief of the temporal and spiritual

30. St. James-the-
Less, Westminster, in
1968 (*Courtauld
Institute*).

31. G. E. Street: St.
James-the-Less,
Westminster (*The
Ecclesiologist*, 1859).

32. St. James-the-
Less, Westminster:
base of tower
(*Courtauld Institute*).

TWO LONDON
CHURCHES

33. St. James-the-Less,
Westminster: east end
(*Courtald Institute*).

34. St. James-the-
Less, Westminster:
model by C. N.
Thwaites in the
church (*photo: James
Austin*).

wants of his fellow men." He built five churches—two on his
Shropshire estate and two, besides St. Martin's, in London—St.
Jude, Collingham Road (designed by George Godwin, 1870–
1871), and St. Matthew Bayswater (designed by John Johnson,
1880). As a churchman he was a strong evangelical.

So here we have these two founders. The pious, affluent
aristocratic high church daughters of a bishop on the one hand;
the successful evangelical glove manufacturer and self-made
country gentleman on the other. The fabrics of the two churches
proclaim at once to anyone familiar with English church architecture of the nineteenth century the social and religious colora-

TWO LONDON
CHURCHES

53

35. (on facing page)
St. James-the-Less,
Westminster, from an
old photograph
(*courtesy of Mrs.
Massey-Miles*).

36. St. James-the-
Less, Westminster
(*The Builder*, 1862).

TWO LONDON
CHURCHES

tion of their founders. But why and how? Clearly it is a matter in the first instance of the choice of architect, and there we are hopelessly baffled for we do not know how the Misses Monk came to hear of Mr. Street, or how Mr. Allcroft came to hear of Mr. Lamb. But let us turn to these architects and consider their careers.

Street was born in 1824, Lamb eighteen years earlier, in 1806. There, in the age difference, at once, is a decisive factor where architectural loyalties are concerned. When Pugin's *Contrasts* appeared in 1836, Lamb was thirty and Street twelve. Both missed, for different reasons, what Gilbert Scott was to call "the awakening." Lamb was too old, already at the drawing board, when Street was born, and he was thirty at the awakening. Street was too young; he blithely inherited the new illumination. Gilbert Scott, between the two, and only seven months older than Pugin, tells us how he "felt like a person awakened from a long, feverish dream." Any Gothic man who was thirty in 1836 as Lamb was had necessarily been in the "feverish dream" so long that it was for him a normal condition. That could be held to explain the curious, highly individual course Lamb's career as a Gothic designer was to follow.

Lamb was the son of a civil servant with a talent for painting.[4] He was articled to L. N. Cottingham, a Gothic enthusiast, one of the first careful restorers, and the creator of a museum in the Waterloo Road which became the nucleus of the Architectural Museum in Tufton Street and eventually part of the collection of Gothic casts at South Kensington. Lamb exhibited at the Royal Academy regularly from the age of eighteen. In or about 1831 (at twenty-five) he got to know John Claudius Loudon and contributed most of the designs for Gothic and Elizabethan furniture and all the villa interiors to the *Encyclopaedia of Cottage, Farm and Villa Architecture* which came out in 1832.[5] Loudon then started the *Architectural Magazine* which ran from 1835 to 1838, and Lamb was one of his principal contributors. It is in the designs he made for the *Encyclopaedia* that we can first identify his peculiar manner, a manner which he developed

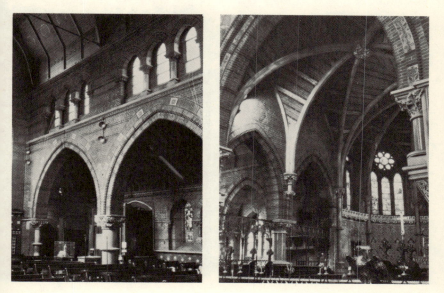

37. (at left) St. James-the-Less, Westminster: nave to northwest *(Courtauld Institute)*.

38. (above) St. James-the-Less, Westminster: chancel to northeast *(Courtauld Institute)*.

with wonderful persistence for thirty years. He is said to have designed between thirty and forty churches as well as many country houses, vicarages, and other things. For Disraeli he built part of Hughenden. At his death in 1869 the *Builder* obituarist called him "an enthusiast in his profession," adding that "he was by no means an architect of the pattern-book school, but constantly endeavoured, even at the expense sometimes of beauty, to exhibit originality."[6] Of this we shall perhaps find confirmation at St. Martin's.

Street was the son of a solicitor and, at sixteen, was given a stool in the family office.[7] He was already a dedicated ecclesiologist, tramping round churches and abbeys with his elder brother. He had obvious artistic talent and little aptitude for

TWO LONDON
CHURCHES

57

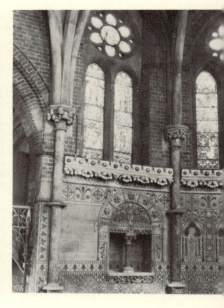

39. (above) St. James-the-Less, Westminster: south transept to north *(Courtauld Institute).*

40. (at right) St. James-the-Less, Westminster: north wall of apse *(Courtauld Institute).*

41. (on facing page) St. James-the-Less, Westminster: north of Chancel arch *(Courtauld Institute).*

TWO LONDON CHURCHES

58

law. This was appreciated by his father who, having the loan of some drawings by Owen Carter, the Winchester architect, exclaimed as he looked through them, "Ah! this would be the very thing for George." It was. He was articled to Carter and was with him for three rather uninspiring years. Then he went to Scott and Moffat where he helped Scott with the St. Nikolaus, Hamburg, drawings. In 1848, at twenty-four, he built his first church—Par in Cornwall—a blameless piece of Early English. In 1850, at twenty-six, he moved to Wantage and in that year went to France for the first time. He toured Germany in 1851,

in 1852 moved to Oxford, married, and went again to France. In 1853 he was in full practice, with Cuddesdon Theological College and St. Peter, Bournemouth, on his hands. In that year also he visited Italy for the first time, saw it through the eyes of Ruskin, and collected the notes and sketches which enabled him to produce his influential *Brick and Marble Architecture in North Italy* in 1855. In 1856 he moved to London and submitted a design in the New Government Offices Competition and received a premium (see p. 87). Philip Webb and Morris, who was living with Burne-Jones, were in his office. This was a moment when Pre-Raphaelitism glowed with promise. Street shared the glow for a little; it was with him when he built the Boyne Hill group at Maidenhead (Fig. 29) and when, in 1858, he was commissioned to build his first London work, the church with which we are now concerned. After that his career took him in charge. He became locked in a professional struggle against time—the rattle of the T-square alternating with the rattle of harness and the rumble of trains. The lists are incomplete, but 263 original works and 360 restorations are recorded. The law Courts, as everybody knows, at last got the better of his fantastic vitality, and he died at fifty-seven in 1881.

Goodhart-Rendel once said to me about Street that he thought of him as "the first Gothic Revivalist who smiled as he worked." Rendel's intuitions were always penetrating but not always easy to put into the prosy terms of art history. I think what Rendel implied was that Street, coming into the Gothic movement *after* the crisis of the thirties, had no barriers to break and no criteria to discover. Pugin, Scott, Pearson, and Butterfield had most earnestly done all that; and there was Ruskin. There was also a growing sense of boredom in the fifties with the first phase of the revival. Pearson's nearly perfect fourteenth-century church at Bessborough Gardens (now destroyed) summarized it all, while Butterfield, at All Saints', Margaret Street, had persuaded the Cambridge Camden Society that innovations, even of foreign provenance, were not only no longer reprehensible but right. So a young architect with a generous church commission on his hands in 1858 could let his imagination play. Street had already done so in his beautiful group of church, schools, and vicarage at Boyne Hill (Fig. 29), though here the play was Butterfieldian. At St. James the Less he claimed further freedoms, enjoyed himself, and delighted nearly everybody.

The church consists of a nave of three bays with clerestory

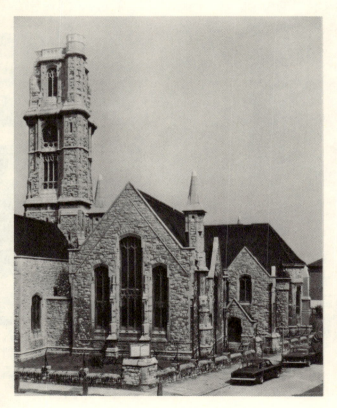

42. St. Martin, Gospel Oak, 1862-1865, from southwest (*Courtauld Institute*).

TWO LONDON CHURCHES

43. St. Martin,
Gospel Oak:
pre-1940 photograph
of tower (*John
Summerson*).

44. (at top) St. Martin, Gospel Oak:
lower part of tower (modern addition
on right) *(Courtauld Institute)*.

45. (at bottom) St. Martin, Gospel
Oak: north entrance under tower
(Courtauld Institute).

46. E. Buckton Lamb:
"Design for a Villa
in the Style of the
Second Class of
Gothic Architecture"
(*The Architectural
Magazine and
Journal*, no. 3, 1836,
p. 456).

and wide north and south aisles; a chancel consisting of one square vaulted bay continuing into an apse with semicircular ending; short transepts opening from the chancel, each transept in two gabled units separated from each other internally by a pair of arches; and a tower standing away from the church at the northwest and connected to it by a short, low gallery, leading to the main (north) doorway. Externally the church is made of red brick laced with black and some stone; the roofs are blue slate. Internally, it is red and black brick again with a variety of other materials.

There are three obvious points to make about this building. First, that it is picturesque; second, that it is to a great extent Butterfieldian; third, that it is in style more foreign than English. St. James's is picturesque. No critic of the time could avoid the word, and there is no reason why we should. It is an attempt to make a radiantly charming and provocative group in an environment of utter drabness. If "picturesque" recalls too strongly a quite other kind of thing belonging to the age of Repton and Nash and Wyatt's Gothic, it must be remembered that Street's

TWO LONDON
CHURCHES

picturesque is fortified by three new factors: a belief in liturgical rectitude, as dictated by the Camden Society; a belief in the nature of building materials and their proper use (Pugin and Ruskin); and an idiomatic command of Gothic forms. If these factors make St. James's more "functional" in respect of use and construction, they in no way diminish its picturesque intentions.

Then the church is Butterfieldian. Not only does the scheme of red brick banded and diapered with black derive from All Saints', Margaret Street (complete and ready for dedication when St. James's was begun), but there is a freedom of proportion throughout which derives from the same master. In addition, all sorts of details in ironwork, tiles, and inlay are clearly inspired by him.

Thirdly, St. James the Less is foreign. This, in assessing why the church was so enthusiastically received in professional circles on its completion in 1862, is perhaps the most important point of the three. Its foreignness was the first thing any critic noticed about it and the starting point of his assessment of it. Gothic was still, in the 1850s, so very much considered a national style that deviations toward foreign styles by English architects were a challenge. In the case of St. James the Less the deviations were those of a man who had himself broken new ground in north Italy, seen and studied things that nobody else had bothered with, and enriched his formal vocabulary in a way which was immediately understood by readers of *The Seven Lamps* and *The Stones of Venice*. Here was an English church, in English materials, glowing with all those qualities which Ruskin had found in medieval Venice. The architect, said the *Ecclesiologist,* "has stepped beyond the mere repetition of English medieval forms, to produce a building in which a free eclectic manipulation of parts has been grafted upon a system of polychromatic construction, having its basis in the fact that London is a brick town."[8] It had in fact English roots. Butterfield, the writer pointed out, had used this sort of "constructive polychromy" but had remained English and northern. Street had

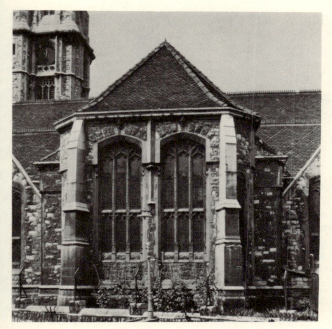

47. St. Martin, Gospel
Oak: south transept
(*Courtauld Institute*).

"drunk deep of the Italian and early French springs" and created
something new. Whatever it was that Street had created new it
was inseparable from his handling and fusing and grafting of
styles, and this is an important point. This obsession with style
and styles, as I pointed out in the first chapter, was central to
the mid-Victorian appreciation of architecture; many of them
felt, even, that it was through the study of style and the fusion
of styles that a modern architecture would make its appearance. It is a question for us to what extent we can now feel the
freshness and excitement of these fusions.

As we approach the church it is the commanding tower

48. St. Martin, Gospel
Oak: interior east
(*Courtauld Institute*).

(Figs. 27, 30, and 31), 134 feet high, which takes our attention
first and in fact directs us to the chief entrance which is in its
base. It rises unbuttressed and sheer, recalling that stern passage
in *The Stones of Venice* where it is enjoined that towers "shall
seem to stand, and shall verily stand, in their own strength, not
by help of buttresses nor artful balancings on this side and on
that."[9] We can also read in the tower a certain scorn for all the
namby-pamby English steeples of the fifties. The style is mostly
Italian till we get to the slate roof, consisting of a low spire and
four attendant spirelets—an idea picked up, I think, in Normandy.
One critic at the time called it "dumpy" and "inharmonious";[10]
another found the spirelets too large.[11] But against this all seem

49. St. Martin, Gospel Oak: interior to northwest *(Courtauld Institute)*.

to have delighted in the exciting play of the horizontal banding against the stark verticals; the nicely judged scale of the openings; the neat transition through a corbel table to the pyramidal roof; and, at the base, the splendid deep brick arches of five orders (Fig. 32), standing over plain splayed jambs and touched into life by the sensitive introduction of a few stone voussoirs and just one order of bricks with serrated edges.

Eastward from the tower extends a little churchyard shown in the engraving (Fig. 27) as fenced from the street by a low wall of pierced brick. This, however, was replaced by a tall iron grille with standards terminating in wrought-iron lilies. Through this is seen the main body of the church, possibly to the modern eye

TWO LONDON CHURCHES

too busy and jerky for so small a building. What, we may ask is that odd gable doing up in the clerestory? The answer to that is that, G. F. Watts having been commissioned to paint a mural over the chancel arch, Street thought of this way of lighting it, though it may also be that he was happy to find an excuse for a quaintly casual gesture in his picturesque ensemble.

The heavily buttressed apse (Fig. 33) is remarkable as almost the only part of the church which is buttressed at all. Because the apse is vaulted and the walls are weakened by large windows, the buttresses are perhaps necessary though they nullify the gracious effect which is the free gift of a shape of this kind.

From other points of view the church is not easy to see or to photograph. However, there is preserved inside it a beautiful little model (Fig. 34) made by a certain C. N. Thwaites which gives an excellent idea of it as Street must have envisaged it. It gives an idea, too, of the sort of color effect at which he aimed —gay, hard, and bright, in contrast to the brown brick and stucco of its environment. A century of London grime and the very up-to-date rebuilding of the adjacent blocks has exactly reversed this effect.

Now, the interior (Figs. 35 and 36). The nave, like that of All Saints', Margaret Street, has three large, handsome bays. They have the effect of establishing a spatial finality which a many-bayed nave cannot have. The brick arches, red and black, spring from double responds with shafts of polished Devonshire marble and meet on squat cylinders of polished Aberdeen granite with Box stone caps and bases and a molded stone band where the granite drums meet (Fig. 37). The blend of styles and materials here is formidable. The *Ecclesiologist's* critic spoke of "a modern Gothic translation of foreign Romanesque" and found "the barbaric bulk" of the columns "striking." But he was not quite happy about them. "There is most unquestionable merit in these pillars, and the world will, we believe, be glad to tolerate them for once or twice in the hand of such an artist as Mr. Street. But . . . in the long run they will not be tolerated." They "will produce a disagreeable revulsion against the revival of good ecclesiastical

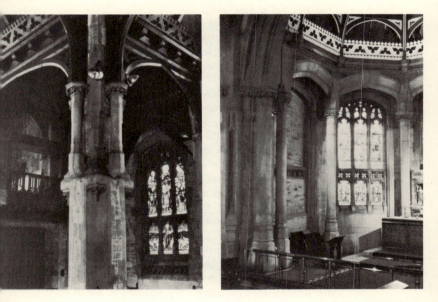

50. (at left) St.
Martin, Gospel Oak:
pier at northwest
corner of crossing
(Courtauld Institute).

51. (above) St.
Martin, Gospel Oak:
north wall of apse
(Courtauld Institute).

architecture. . . . Say what we will, the 19th is not the ninth or
the eleventh century."[12] (As a matter of fact it was not the
thirteenth or fourteenth, but let that pass). Other critics found
the bright red walls "almost too powerful" and "too vivid."[13]

The nave is very high for its width and is covered by a de-
cidedly Butterfieldian cradle roof, painted with the ancestors of
Christ—a sort of Jesse tree—by Clayton and Bell, from designs
by Street. The commissioning of G. F. Watts to paint the space
above the chancel arch was not a great success.[14] Neither Watts's
style of drawing nor his Venetian Renaissance coloring went with
anything else. Everything else was ruled by Street's hand and eye.
He designed the tile work in the aisles and the capitals which

incorporate carved representations of the miracles of Christ. Clayton and Bell did the glass.

The chancel arch is lifted on stumpy marble colonettes standing in turn on brackets (Fig. 41), a deliberate gesture intended to give a feeling of participation by the nave congregation in the proceedings in the chancel. The very low screen has the same intent.

The chancel is vaulted and opens on both sides to the transeptal spaces with their cross arches (Fig. 39)—"infinitely picturesque" said the *Ecclesiologist*. Here the decoration becomes exceedingly rich with inlaid mastic designs on the walls and tile and marble patterns on the floor (Figs. 38 and 40). Here again there is the influence of Butterfield, in the combined play of geometrical patterns with motifs taken from medieval sources. The reredos is made up of inlaid representations of eight holy women in the style of Flemish or German brasses while the central cross is of varicolored Irish marbles, set with studs of Derbyshire spar.

Street's immense talent as a graphic artist is behind all this and behind all the carving everywhere. The carving is, of course, just carving and never crosses the frontier into sculpture. Farmer and Brindley rose gallantly to the occasion in the intricate task set them by Street in the pulpit, which is one entire complex of biblical scenes; but it is still, alas, only carving.

I hope I have made it clear that the whole of this church is an adventure with styles: Butterfieldian, early French, and north Italian crossing and recrossing, fusing and blending in a pattern which reaches its utmost brilliance in the bell stage of the tower and the decoration of the apse. Of the absolute success of the adventure it is hard to judge. Much of the excitement belongs irrevocably to the sixties and was, in fact, beginning to be mocked ten years after the church was built.[15] On the other hand Street's artistry, his handling, does seem to me to transcend the limited interest of the style game and to speak nearly as eloquently now as it did a hundred years ago.

To turn from St. James the Less to St. Martin's is to enter a quite different world of thought and feeling. I have just spoken of Street's artistry, his handling. At St. Martin's these are expressions which one is not at all inclined to use. There is, however, a good deal else.

St. Martin's is, in essence, a central-space church based on a square within which four piers support the timber roof. The four piers, however, are not equidistant so that there is a decisive nave-and-aisles effect and the nave is prolonged westward. To the east is an apsidal sanctuary, octagonal within and without. A vestry is tacked on to the northeast corner, and at the northwest corner of the square is a tower 130 feet high with two openings at its base leading to the main (north) doorway. The placing of this tower and its use as an outer porch is the one feature which St. Martin's has in common with St. James the Less, and it is just possible that Lamb took the idea from the younger man. The materials of the exterior are Kentish rag with Bath stone for the openings and diapered tile roofs. Internally the walls are faced with Hassock stone and the woodwork is stained and varnished pine.[16]

In speaking of St. James the Less, I offered three points as being helpful to an understanding of it—its picturesqueness, its debt to Butterfield, and its foreignness. St. Martin's is certainly picturesque. As to the other two points it is necessary to say not only that it is totally un-Butterfieldian but also that it owes absolutely nothing to any other living architect. Nor is it foreign; its sources, so far as one can unravel them from the mannered distortions, are purely English. St. Martin's is picturesque. But the picturesque here is in direct descent from the age of Nash, Repton, and, of course, John Claudius Loudon and his circle. Its beginnings, in fact, can be found in designs made by Lamb for Loudon's *Encyclopedia* and the *Architectural Magazine* when he was twenty-five or twenty-six (Fig. 46). They are terrifyingly crude, and one would be inclined to dismiss them as blushfully unhappy *juvenilia* which the young man having published would at once outgrow. Not a bit of it. Some of the designs are in the very style he was still expounding at fifty-two.

Lamb was perfectly conscious of the way he was using the picturesque tradition and expresses himself most clearly in the observations accompanying his *Studies of Ancient Domestic Architecture* (1846). He despised the "Gothic" and "castellated" shams of the early years of the century. The essentials of the picturesque, he wrote are "contrast, irregularity, and inequality." On the other hand "the convenient distribution of the apartments should be the foundation of the picturesque . . . in this principle alone can the picturesque be considered beautiful."[17] Street, I suppose, would have agreed with this, and his vicarages conform with the principle most admirably. The difference is that Lamb, when he brings it into church architecture, does so in a pragmatic way whereas Street would accept it for churches only on a liturgical, Camdenian level. The difference is one not only of architectural temperament but also of churchmanship and perhaps in the last resort of social class. One must add, of course, that the difference in form of expression is immeasurable.

Street was an eclectic, an adventurer in styles; Lamb was totally against eclecticism. His belief was that "the very latest Gothic or best Tudor might [but for the Renaissance] have been carried on much longer, and would have acquired fresh spirit and energy. By *continuing* the same spirit which marked the works of preceding ages, we should in a short time work out a style accommodated to our requirements, and at the same time marked by aesthetic quality."[18] Throughout his career he adhered consistently to this idea of the prolongation of late Perpendicular into the nineteenth century not by copying (which he despised) but by re-creating in a new nineteenth-century image. The newness of the image was a matter of "character" (that favorite Victorian word). "The architect," he wrote, "must be able to command character of the express kind and degree suitable to the occasion."[19]

Describing the style of St. Martin's the *Builder* of 1866 no doubt takes its line from the architect himself: "The style . . . is that which was in general use at the time of Henry VII; but the building must be considered rather as a characteristic expression of that style, than as a reproduction, for it would be difficult to find an absolute precedent for any portion of the work."[20] True.

The visitor to St. Martin's will find his attention at once riveted to the tower (Figs. 28, 42, and 43). At its base are two openings (one now unfortunately obscured by the addition of a chapel). These openings excavate the masonry in a series of receding planes so the tower is left standing on legs (Figs. 44 and 45). On these it heaves up to the bell stage where the clockface is impaneled above a three-light opening. Then comes a string course so massive that it would seem to stop everything. But there is another great heave and up we go through a further stage to the pinnacled summit (the pinnacles, alas!, disappeared after bomb damage). I know few towers so tormenting as this one in proportion, modeling, and silhouette. Most towers answer a question. This one asks.

The church itself is, from outside, a rather bewildering collocation of forms, though one can see that on the basis of Lamb's theory of character and the picturesque it works out pretty well. He has adopted a thoroughly sound plan (Fig. 28) enabling a congregation of a thousand to participate in a service at the altar. The vertical projection of this plan he has dealt with piecemeal in terms of gable ends, hipped roofs, eaves, and parapets (Figs. 42 and 47). At whatever point you stand there is an eminently picturesque assemblage of forms—picturesque precisely in the terms specified by the architect—"contrast, irregularity, and inequality." As for character one must, I think, admire at least the consistency of Lamb's intensely mannered interpretation of Perpendicular. It is harsh, angular, and intricate; but all of it speaks the same language, from the lofty stabilizing pinnacles which terminate in miniature broach spires down to the ornamental buttresses with their tiny splays and penetrations. And it is all exactly the language of the tower.

Only one feature of the exterior explains what the interior is going to be like, and that is the overwhelming expanse of tiled roof. Sure enough, on entering the church one is less aware of the masonry structure than of a forest of varnished pine carpentry gathered overhead (Figs. 48 and 49). It takes the form of a hammer-beam roof going from end to end of the nave and turning at right angles into the transepts, so that at the central space there is a tentlike effect with long diagonal rafters. The main points of support are the four masonry columns of the central space (Fig. 50). These are designed in the strangest way and in a way close in spirit to the tower. Each column starts on a square pier chamfered nearly to an octagon then returning to square. Above the square, on each face, comes an inward splay and out of each splay comes a shaft—out and up to a carved capital which in turn carries the spandril piece either of a hammer beam or one of the cross beams of the lesser openings. The effect of heaving up the roof is in its way as dramatic as the upward heave of the tower from stage to stage. The roof itself is plainly, not to say crudely, detailed. Indeed the whole interior is hard and plain. Even the apsidal sanctuary (Fig. 51) is severe and was very much more so before successive modifications brought it to the more or less typical Anglican compromise which it presents today. There was, however, always stained glass.[21] There was no high church nonsense about John Derby Allcroft. He had the royal arms carved (and rather well carved) over the south door and the Lord's Prayer and Commandments exhibited in Gothic panels on either side of the chancel arch.

St. Martin's was received with respect rather than enthusiasm by the *Builder*[22] and amiably by the critic of the *Companion to the Almanac* who always had a sympathetic feeling for Lamb.[23] Both were intrigued by the now rare adoption of Perpendicular. The *Ecclesiologist,* however, administered the greatest snub in its power: it said nothing. We know what the *Ecclesiologist* thought of Edward Buckton Lamb because it had reviewed his Christ Church, West Hartlepool, exhibited at the R. A. ten years previously, in these terms: "one of those uncouth and grotesque combinations of incongruous architectural *tours de force* which it requires the inartistic and withal presumptuous mind of Mr. Lamb to conceive."[24] But they had detected the wolf in Mr. Lamb five years before that when they noticed a sketch of a church by him in the Architectural Exhibition as looking "very ghastly."[25] Eastlake, in his *History of the Gothic Revival* of 1872 lists, in his long and valuable appendix, not a single church by Lamb—another snub, this time posthumous.

The first modern eye to notice that Lamb was a serious and original performer was Goodhart-Rendel's. In his vastly entertaining paper on "Rogue Architects of the Victorian Era" (1949)[26] he describes St. Martin's as "a completely original and, I think, almost perfect, solution of what a large auditorium for protestant services should be." Of Lamb's idiosyncratic details he is tolerant: "Parts of them are excellent and none of them really turn me up." Nikolaus Pevsner, I notice, in the course of his peregrinations has been bowled over more than once by Lamb's churches; he picks himself up looking rather guilty and murmurs "perverse," "mischievous." In 1952 he wrote of St. Martin's as "the craziest of London's Victorian churches."[27]

I am not trying to convert anybody to Lamb or indeed to Street or anybody else. What interests me is the situation in which two such wholly different churches as St. James the Less and St. Martin's could be produced almost simultaneously—both by the agency of philanthropic churchmanship. Also why, of these two highly original works, one flourished in the sunshine of fashionable approval and the other sank quickly through disfavor to oblivion. The first question I think I have already partly answered. It was not just temperament that made Lamb a "rogue" architect. It was the accident of birth: he matured too early to be a "proper" Gothic revivalist. Or, if you like, he made—before Pugin came on the scene—a Gothic revival of his own and had the courage and pertinacity to stick to it. Street, so much younger, was carried at once on the flowing tide of fashionable high church art in which he brilliantly swam to fame. The other matter, that of esteem and its opposite, is much more difficult. It is a question of the linkage between artistic criteria, churchmanship, wealth, and social class—a problem in the history of patronage.

But perhaps the most interesting thing of all is how we

receive these churches in our own modern minds—making as we do so something different of them, betraying, distorting their designers' intention, and then trying very hard to put things right by being good art historians, quoting contemporary documents and texts. Forty-five years ago when I was a student nobody except Goodhart-Rendel had the slightest curiosity about these churches. Now they are again talked of. And they come back so oddly. I am sure that today Lamb, whose forms seem so often bizarre and without precedent, has the edge over Street, for whose forms precedents can usually be found if you look hard enough. There is, perhaps, even an exact reversal here. Street was, in a sense you will recognize, an "artistic" architect. Lamb was, let us admit, pretty "inartistic." Both were intelligent and inventive. But Street's invention is inseparable from that process which I have referred to so often—the drawing together of evocative elements from various epochs to constitute a "style" for a particular nineteenth-century occasion. In this process, for us, the warmth of fresh discovery, fusion, or juxtaposition is almost irrecoverable. Lamb is cruder, much cruder; but his style is a consistent, if highly personal, interpretation of late English Gothic and his originalities therefore strike us more readily, shock us more. And it would be idle to pretend that in the course of our revaluation of Victorian architecture we do not sometimes find it agreeable rather than otherwise to be shocked.

IV. A Victorian Competition:
The Royal Courts of Justice

COMPETITIONS for major public buildings begin to be formally organized in England at the same time that the architectural profession itself begins to show a self-conscious corporate identity, and this is about the beginning of Victoria's reign. These competitions attracted spectacular concentrations of effort. What came out of a competition and got built is sometimes scarcely more important for the historian than what went into the competition and did not get built. Designs other than the winner's often made a great impact. The public, too, watched and marveled. Architecture was, for once, on the stage, offering itself for applause or ridicule. A competition gave the opportunity to compare; and the great competitions where enough designs have been preserved still give us, in a unique way, this opportunity of evaluating by means of comparisons on a firm datum.

That part of Victoria's reign with which I am concerned in this book saw the most exciting competitions of the century. Two years before the reign opened, in 1835, there had been the Houses of Parliament competition, won by Charles Barry. In 1838 came the Royal Exchange competition; in 1856 the Public Offices competition; in 1859 the Manchester Assize Courts competition; in 1864 the South Kensington Museum competition; and in 1866–1867 two major competitions—that for a new National

Gallery in Trafalgar Square and that for the Royal Courts of
Justice on a site in the Strand. It is the last of these which is the
main subject of this chapter but in approaching it I want to
mention two of the earlier competitions—those for the Houses
of Parliament and the Government Offices in Whitehall. One
reason why I group these two with the last is that all three were
promoted by the Government and were for buildings of conspicuous national importance. A deeper reason is that all three
conspicuously involved that question which is a key to the
understanding of this period, the question of style.

The Houses of Parliament competition of 1835 was con-
sequent upon the burning of the old Palace of Westminster in
the previous year. It was by far the most formal and carefully
organized architectural contest ever held in England at that date.
Competitors were supplied with full details of the requirements
as formulated by the Committees for both Houses of Parliament
and even with a positive instruction regarding style. This was

contained in a resolution of the Committees: "that the style of the buildings be Gothic or Elizabethan."[1]

There were ninety-seven entries for this competition and the winner was Charles Barry (Fig. 52). His plan was recognized as perfectly complete and convenient, but what dazzled the judges and undoubtedly was the deciding factor in Barry's favor was his mastery of Gothic detail.[2] Whether Pugin had given him much help at this stage—it is, in my view, unlikely—does not matter. The point is that the greatest Government building of all had been decided largely on a question of the imitation and handling of the Gothic style.

The second great Government competition came twenty-one years later, in 1856. It was a triple competition, with separate awards for two large blocks of building to rehouse two greatly swollen departments of state—the War Office and the Foreign Office—and, in addition, an award for a site plan for both buildings. This competition, too, was organized on a grand scale and this time it was not confined to Englishmen. Foreigners were allowed to compete and designs came—though not many—from Paris, Munich, Vienna, and America. Two hundred and eighteen designs were submitted. No explicit directions were given as to style, but a story got round that the Government would certainly not look at anything which was not in some kind of classical style. Thus, among the 218 designs submitted, only nineteen were Gothic, two of these being from Germany. None of the Gothic designs received a first award in either competition, which perhaps proved the rumor correct. Five, however, did receive minor awards.[3]

The winning designs in the first lists were by almost unknown young architects who had looked long and hard at Visconti's new Louvre. Coe and Hofland were first for the War Office,[4] and H. B. Garling was first for the Foreign Office.[5] Their designs were of a type which might have cropped up anywhere in Europe—or, indeed, America—at this date. Banks and Barry, second in the Foreign Office list, naturally followed the Italian style of Barry's father, the great Sir Charles.[6] Rochead of Glasgow sent in a full-blooded Sansovinesque design merging into "modern French".[7] The only other "Italian" design of much distinction was that of Cuthbert Brodrick of Leeds, fifth in the War Office list.[8] He had been trained in Paris, but time had passed and his noble mass of columnar Neoclassicism was just about thirty years out of date.

Of those who dared to adventure in Gothic we have the names of only five—the five who in the first published decisions received premiums, namely: in the Foreign Office list, George Gilbert Scott (third), Deane and Woodward (fourth), Buxton and

53. Deane and Woodward: early design for the Museum of Physical Sciences, Oxford (*The Builder*, 1855).

54. Public Offices Competition, 1856. G. Gilbert Scott: design for Foreign Office (*R. I. B. A. Library*).

55. Public Offices Competition, 1856. G. Gilbert Scott: design for War Office (*R. I. B. A.*).

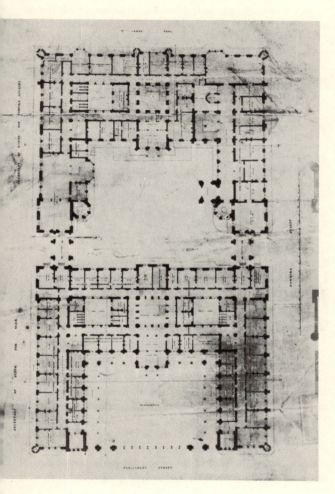

56. Public Offices
Competition, 1856.
G. Gilbert Scott:
plans of War Office
(lower part) and
Foreign Office (upper
part) (*R. I. B. A.
Library*).

A VICTORIAN
COMPETITION

Habershon (sixth), and George Edmund Street (seventh); and in the War Office list, Prichard and Seddon (fourth).

Of these five, one may immediately be dismissed: the design of Buxton and Habershon was merely a conventional if painstaking Gothic dress-up of a plan for which they also offered an Italian version.[9] The remaining four were all works of the English medievalist *avant garde*, wholly committed to the Gothic cause. Scott was the oldest at forty-five. Woodward (the effective

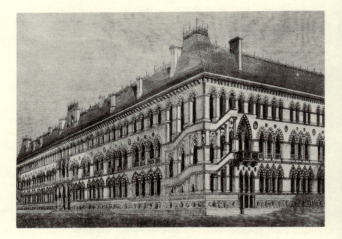

57. Public Offices Competition, 1856. Deane and Woodward: design for Foreign Office (*Illustrated London News*, 1857).

partner in Deane and Woodward) was forty-one, Street thirty-two, and Seddon (of Prichard and Seddon) twenty-nine. Of these, three were to be competitors in the Law Courts competition ten years later, and their designs are therefore relevant to my main subject. Woodward was to die in 1861, leaving the younger Deane to compete, all too ineffectively, on his own account.

We have sadly inadequate records of these Gothic designs (except Scott's, whose drawings survive), but their interest as

58. Public Offices
Competition, 1856.
G. E. Street: design
for Foreign Office
(*Illustrated London
News*, 1857).

59. Public Offices
Competition, 1856.
Prichard and Seddon:
design for War Office
(*Building News*,
1857).

the first serious approach of the Gothic movement to the problem of a first-class public building is great. All turn their backs,
of course, on the Palace of Westminster, now a bogey—everything that modern Gothic architecture should not be: late, flat,
corrupt. The only modern secular Gothic buildings of any relevance at this date were either domestic or collegiate; the only
building of "public" character was the Museum of Physical Sciences at Oxford, designed by Deane and Woodward under the

60. Law Courts
Competition, 1866.
G. Gilbert Scott: the
Strand Front.

61. Law Courts
Competition, 1866.
G. Gilbert Scott: the
Great Ambulatory.

immediate influence, both as to ideas and actual forms, of *The Stones of Venice*. This was still in progress, but a view was published in 1855 (Fig. 53).[10] Two of the significant Gothic designs in the Public Offices competition reflect its influence; a third is the work of the same architects.

George Gilbert Scott showed the influence of the Oxford Museum very clearly in the park front of his Foreign Office block (the design for which he was premiated) with its high-roofed central tower (Fig. 54). But the plan (Fig. 56) is a three-sided courtyard affair which could as easily have been interpreted in Neoclassical as in Gothic terms. His War Office (not premiated), sited between the Foreign Office and Whitehall, was almost a duplicate of this, with a screen toward Whitehall which could quite easily have been interpreted in terms of Holland or Nash (Fig. 55). On these far from revolutionary plans Scott raised elevations of richly picturesque Gothic character, mostly from French sources but with some Italian polychromy.[11] He describes his approach with complete candor:

I . . . set myself to design the elements which I thought best suited to a public building. I designed windows suited to all positions, and of all varieties of size, form and grouping; doorways, cornices, parapets and imaginary combinations of all three, carefully studying to make them all practical, and suited to this class of building.[12]

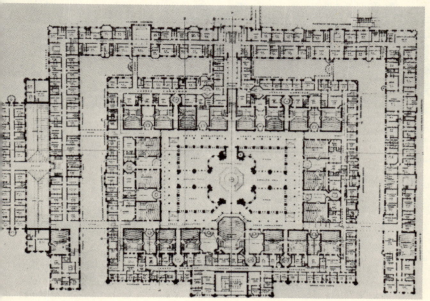

62. Law Courts Competition, 1866. G. Gilbert Scott: plan at Court level.

63. Law Courts
Competition, 1866.
H. F. Lockwood: the
Strand front.

This is a remarkable confession of what "style" meant to Scott and, indeed, many of his contemporaries—it meant, in effect, a sum of details. The plan was something else. It needed, of course, to be practical and a practical plan often turned out not wholly unlike a traditional Neoclassical plan. And why not? The "art" was in the ornaments.

Of the other three designs we have, most unfortunately, no plans and must judge their authors' intentions by perspective views alone and these in sketchy wood-engraved versions. Deane and Woodward (fourth in the Foreign Office list) show an extraordinarily original conception with an elevation to the Park of strongly Venetian character with open built-in staircases at

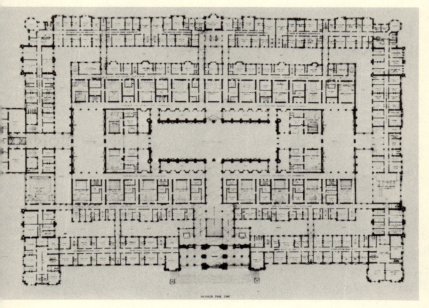

either end. (Fig. 57).[13] A separately published detail[14] shows that
the architects adhered to their Oxford (and Ruskinian) ideal of
integrating architecture and sculpture and were to cover much
of the exterior with historical reliefs in an archaic style. The design was praised by Ruskin.[15]

Street (seventh in the Foreign Office list) was even less
orthodox. He saw the Foreign and War Offices united as a
collegiate complex with every sort of picturesque irregularity and
an elegant tower rising somewhere in the midst (Fig. 58).[16] The
Building News critic found it all "as free and sketchy as the style
will allow"[17] and complained of the impracticability of broken
floor levels. The *Builder* wondered if such determined irregularity

A VICTORIAN
COMPETITION

87

65. Law Courts
Competition. 1866.
J. A. Brandon: view
from northwest.

was even good Gothic.[18] Street had lately returned from his
north Italian tour and in the details of his design his experiences
are faithfully reflected.

Prichard and Seddon (fourth in the War Office list), like
Scott, found the Oxford Museum to provide an irresistible clue
for the Park front; but they followed the Oxford building further
in articulating some elements in the program quite separately
from the main block (Fig. 59).[19] Just as the Oxford Museum has
a satellite laboratory in the shape, approximately, of the Abbot's
kitchen at Glastonbury, so Seddon's Foreign Office has a satellite
chateau for the Secretary of State and, in addition, a satellite

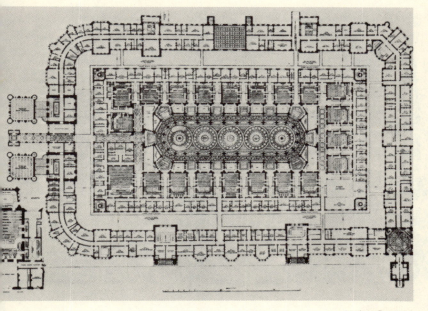

66. Law Courts
Competition, 1866.
J. A. Brandon: plan
at Court level.

stable for the chateau. His style derives partly from the Oxford Museum (i.e., Venetian) and partly from France.

We have already seen that this famous competition was won by two little-known architects with conventional designs in the latest style from Paris. But winning a competition could be a very long way from being appointed executant architect. There were powerful people, some of them in Parliament, who were determined that the new Offices should be Gothic. An investigation of the awards was instituted and confidential lists discovered, prepared by the professional advisers to the board of assessors, somewhat different from the official lists. In each of these

67. Law Courts
Competition, 1866.
G. E. Street: bird's-
eye view.

confidential lists the name of George Gilbert Scott was placed
second. From this a Parliamentary Committee drew the quaint
conclusion that having been placed second in the two confidential lists, Scott must be a better man than anyone placed
first either in those lists or the ones promulgated by the entire
board. Scott was therefore appointed. The Gothic cause pre-
vailed, but not for long. Palmerston, coming into power in 1859,
set his face firmly against Gothic, scrambled the whole issue, and
made Scott build a building in orthodox and by no means ig-
noble Italian classic.[20]

The impact of the Public Offices competition, through the
exhibition in Westminster Hall, the publication of designs in

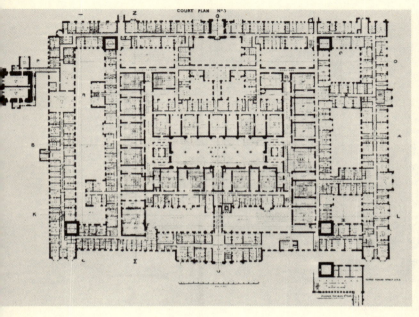

68. Law Courts
Competition, 1866.
G. E. Street: plan at
Court level.

the building press and the inclusion of some of the designs in
the Royal Academy exhibition, was very great. It could even be
said that the competition, in spite of its total failure as a direct
means of obtaining what the Queen's Government wanted, es-
tablished an image of monumental secular Gothic architecture
which persisted for two decades and more. Thus in 1859 a competition was held for new Assize Courts in Manchester. It was
won by an unknown architect of twenty-nine, Alfred Waterhouse.
His design owed much to the Whitehall efforts of Scott and
perhaps of Seddon, and it was actually built.[21] Its completion in
1864 not only launched him on his tremendous career but
rendered him conspicuously eligible for the competition which

A VICTORIAN
COMPETITION

91

69. Law Courts
Competition, 1866.
G. E. Street: the
Public Hall.

70. (at right) Law
Courts Competition,
1866. G. E. Street:
alternative design for
Record Tower.

A VICTORIAN
COMPETITION

92

is our main preoccupation here, that for the Royal Courts of
Justice, initiated in 1866.

The prehistory of this competition has a certain bearing on
the architecture it produced.[22] As early as 1832, before the
burning of the old Palace of Westminster, the removal of the
courts from around Westminster Hall, where Soane had only
lately rebuilt them, had been seriously proposed. After the
fire of 1834, the old courts—unburnt, still clinging round Westminster Hall, but incapable of further expansion—were seen
to be obsolescent and in 1842 Charles Barry made a design for
a new building of a Neoclassical kind, sited in the middle of
Lincoln's Inn Fields. Mercifully this was abandoned. In 1858
further steps were taken to find a site, and the choice fell on

an area of poor and ancient houses between the Strand and Carey Street. In 1865 came the Acts for acquiring the land and building on it, and early in the following year invitations were sent to certain architects to submit designs in competition. An international deluge of architectural paper was not, on this occasion, envisaged. Some of the invited architects declined, further invitations were sent and, in the end, eleven of the most distinguished practitioners in the country undertook the task of designing what, after the Palace of Westminster, would be the most important new public building of the Victorian century. Each competitor was guaranteed a fee of £800. The architects were H. R. Abraham, E. M. Barry, Raphael Brandon, William Burges, T. N. Deane, H. B. Garling, H. F. Lockwood, J. P. Seddon, G. Gilbert Scott, G. E. Street, and Alfred Waterhouse. Of these, Scott and Lockwood were the oldest at fifty-six, E. M. Barry and Alfred Waterhouse the youngest at thirty-seven. Garling, Seddon, Scott, and Street had, as we have seen, been premiated in the Government Offices competition; so had Deane when he was in partnership with Woodward who, however, had died in 1861. Abraham was included on the strength of a plan he had already made for the new Courts in 1857, at the behest of his brother-in-law, the Attorney General. The plan served as a sort of pilot scheme for the other competitors and Abraham's participation as one of them (with another design) was never taken seriously. E. M. Barry was an inevitable choice as the rising star of the Barry dynasty and already, at thirty-seven, the architect of Covent Garden Opera-house and two huge hotels. Raphael Brandon, known chiefly for his cathedral-like edifice in Gordon Square, was an unexpected choice. So, perhaps, was Burges who, however, had the distinction of having won the international competition for Lille Cathedral in 1856 and that for the Memorial Church at Constantinople in 1857. Lockwood was an eminent provincial working in Bradford. Waterhouse, another provincial, was, of course, the widely acclaimed architect of the Assize Courts at Manchester which even the judicial authorities had found satisfactory.

71. Law Courts
Competition, 1866.
W. Burges: bird's-eye
view.

The conditions were drawn up with meticulous care and
in the greatest possible detail. It was made clear to competitors
that the designs would be judged wholly on questions of convenience and efficiency and without respect to style or artistic intention—which, it was no doubt assumed, the rank from which
the competitors were drawn would in any case supply. (Nevertheless, the almost sadistic force with which this condition was
expressed reflects the suspicion with which architects were
regarded by authority at this juncture.) Of course, the art question—which is to say, the style question—was at no stage avoid-
able. The Law Courts competition, unlike the Public Offices
competition was, by the competitors' own choice, a Gothic com-

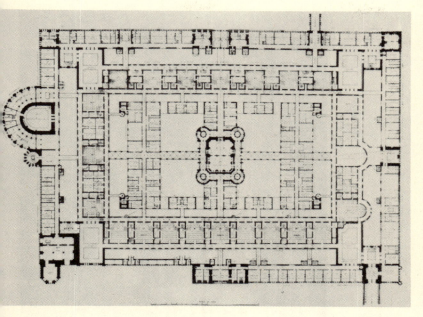

petition from the start. Architects of mainly Italian inclination either declined to compete (T. H. Wyatt and P. C. Hardwick) or dropped out later (John Gibson) leaving only fully armed Goths in the field. An exception was H. B. Garling, who showed his distrust of the situation and his own capacities by submitting a round-arched alternative to his Gothic scheme. Nothing much was heard of either.

Why this assumption that the new Law Courts would be Gothic? There are two likely answers. One is that, historically and topographically, the Law Courts issued from Westminster and Westminster had always been and still were Gothic—even though not now in any of the kinds of Gothic currently ap-

73. Law Courts
Competition, 1866.
W. Burges: the
Judges' Hall.

A VICTORIAN
COMPETITION

96

proved. Another, more immediate, answer was that most of the architects of the right age to be invited (i.e., experienced, but not too old to carry the undertaking through in their lifetimes) had been caught young by the Gothic movement and had practiced nothing else. These architects would, I think, have added a third reason: that only the infinitely flexible Gothic style could solve the problem of piling such a vast quantity of accommodation on so restricted a space. The competition thus hit a unique moment in English architecture. Palmerston's decision and Scott's surrender at Whitehall had discouraged nobody, though some thought the worse of Scott. In any case, the exhibition of the eleven designs, which opened in a specially erected gallery in New Square, Lincoln's Inn, in 1867, was an exhibition of Gothic and, indeed, a harvest of mid-Victorian Gothic invention such as had never been seen before and would never be seen again.[23]

Competitors were directed by the instructions and by Abraham's pilot plan to the idea that the only possible way of dealing with the accommodation was in a series of concentric rectangles. This excluded at once the kind of organic axial planning which any competent Frenchman would automatically have adopted. It invited a more intimate and involute handling, more congenial, perhaps, to Gothic thinking. Putting aside the innumerable problems of detailed disposition (there were 1,304 rooms), there was one great issue confronting the competitors which radically affected the whole architectural result—whether or not to introduce a great central hall and if so what shape to make it. No ceremonial hall, no *salle-des-pas-perdus*, was called for in the conditions, which insisted simply and severely on the segregation of the various users of the building. But segregation can only be achieved with proper circulation and how could any system of circulation work without some sort of central rendezvous? The competitors were driven to some hard thinking. This rendezvous could be made the central approach to the courts, but as a minimum of 24 courts was required it would either have to be an enormously wasteful circular or multilateral

74. Law Courts
Competition, 1866.
J. P. Seddon: model
(southeast aspect).

75. Law Courts
Competition, 1866.
J. P. Seddon: plan at
Court level.

76. (on facing page)
Law Courts
Competition, 1866.
J. P. Seddon: the
Great Hall.

77. Law Courts
Competition, 1866.
A. Waterhouse: the
Strand front.

space or else so long and thin as to be more of a monumental corridor.

The second main challenge was the architectural one: how to bring Gothic feeling and scholarship to bear on this enormous mass of building, how to compose it into an intrinsically Gothic unity, and most especially how to manage the conspicuous Strand front. This would be 276 yards long. The only modern Gothic precedent for a front of such length was the 300 yards long river front of Barry's Houses of Parliament. That was now despised for being Grecian under the skin. Was it possible to avoid this sort of symmetrical build-up and if so how? The answer involved, of course, the whole conception of the plan and the whole idea of what Gothic could mean when applied to a highly organized modern building of strictly utilitarian purpose (so the conditions implied) and of enormous size?

There were, of course, plenty of other problems besides

these two—notably the problem of levels—but if, in a brief review, we investigate how some of the competitors tried to solve these two we shall gain some insight into the workings of the architectural mind at one of the most critical moments in English architecture. There are obviously good reasons for reviewing the designs in the order dictated by their authors' age. We start therefore with George Gilbert Scott and H. F. Lockwood, both fifty-seven.

George Gilbert Scott's[24] plan (Fig. 62) has an internal street enclosing a center block on three sides with the Strand on the fourth. The main feature of his center block is a double ambulatory (Fig. 61) forming an inner rectangle. From this ambula-

78. Law Courts Competition, 1866. A. Waterhouse: plan at principal floor level (below Court level).

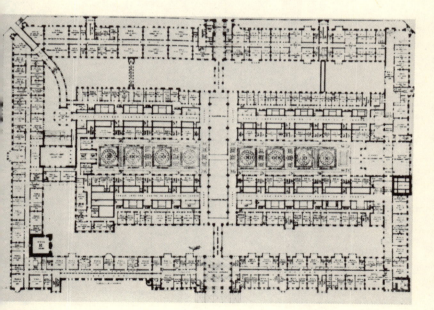

79. Law Courts
Competition, 1866.
A. Waterhouse: the
Central Hall.

80. Law Courts Competition, 1866. A. Waterhouse: the Transverse Halls.

tory nearly but not quite all the courts are reached. In the hollow rectangle of the ambulatory is an octagonal central hall with a great octagonal staircase; another, circular, staircase within it and at the very center a lift; staircases and lift rising only to the court floor. The hall itself is covered by a dome carried on eight arches and having flat surfaces for mural paintings. It is an original and interesting plan with Neoclassical roots, most industriously concealed, however, by a stylistic handling which sways gently between Gothic and Byzantine. Neoclassical

A VICTORIAN
COMPETITION

at root is also the Strand front (Fig. 60). A composition of this kind with projecting center, two towers and side wings is close to Durand;[25] but the Gothic treatment carries us to the Doge's Palace and, in the center, the Brussels town hall. The middle projection is not, as one might think, a great hall; the center is occupied by one of the appellate courts and there is a chamber to each side of it. The towers exhibit a clock and a sundial respectively but their main purpose is ventilation. In short the majesty of the Strand front is rather contrived.

81. Law Courts
Competition, 1866.
E. M. Barry: the
Strand front.

Scott had, of late years, learnt from Lord Palmerston to be accommodating about style. "I should be quite ready," he writes in his report, "if thought too ornate, to adopt a severer tone." He would go as far as round arches. He even submitted a design for an alternative hall with an iron roof.

H. F. Lockwood,[26] the Bradford architect, has a churchlike hall insulated in the middle of the building and with poor access to the courts (Fig. 64). His symmetrical Strand front (Fig 63) gathers enormous emphasis at the center, singularly inappropriate to the narrow Strand. The main source is Barry's river front at Westminster, an enlarged version of Barry's clock tower being dumped in the center of the whole.

Raphael Brandon,[27] like Lockwood, introduced a churchlike hall in the middle of his plan (Fig. 66), but with better access to the courts. The attractiveness of this plan is probably due to

82. Law Courts
Competition, 1866.
E. M. Barry: plan at
Court level.

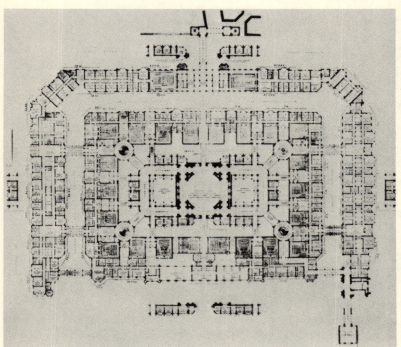

83. (on facing page)
G. E. Street: the
Law Courts, London.
The Great Hall, 1874-
78 (*National
Monuments Record*).

84. G. E. Street: the
Law Courts, London.
Detail of Strand
entrance, 1874-78
(*National Monuments
Record*).

A VICTORIAN
COMPETITION

Brandon's early training under an architect of the Beaux Arts School. The hall is enormously high, like a vast Sainte Chapelle; its interior, however, turns out to be almost indistinguishable from Westminster Abbey except that it is twice the size and has an apse at both ends. The Strand front is a clear derivative from Barry but jumped-up in the middle. The west front (Fig. 65) makes a fabulous spectacle in the perspective but the total effect is that of a cathedral gone wrong. This is the kind of

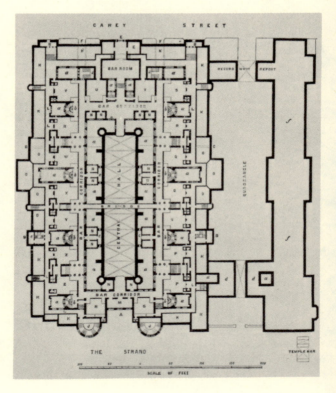

85. G. E. Street: plan of the Law Courts as executed.

86. (on facing page) J. Poelaert: Palais de Justice, Brussels, 1866-83.

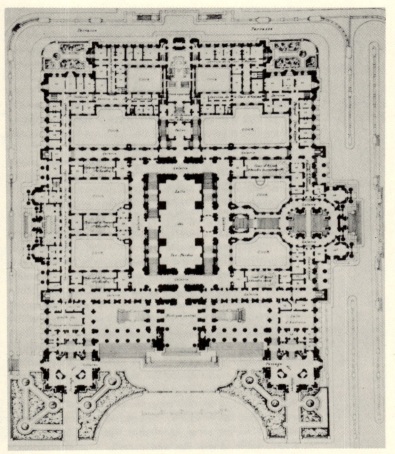

"copyist" romancing which the Gothic Revival is often supposed to be but so rarely is.

George Edmund Street[28] submitted a design (Figs. 67 to 70) very complex both in plan and section. The dominating feature is, once again, a vaulted hall, but Street, conceiving it as a monumental corridor rather than a place of assembly, stressed it lengthwise by introducing a central arcade. This great hall or corridor is approached by a vaulted stair with no direct access from the street; it admits, furthermore, only to the galleries of the courts, the merely curious public being thus trapped in Gothic aisles from which they could take gallery views of the course of justice without possibility of contact with those concerned with it. The latter have their separate entrances and approach the courts by way of a vaulted undercroft. Although this arrangement answers one of the problems posed, it results in a terribly puzzling and even rather nightmarish plan. Street's Strand elevations reflect the symmetry of the plan but in a gentle, casual, Gothic way and without any dramatic build-up at the center. Drama is reserved for the stupendous record tower (Fig. 70) at the northwest corner.

William Burges[29] brings us to the under-forties. Anyone knowing Burges would know that he would "act medieval" to a preposterous extent, and one wonders why he was invited to participate in a competition as full of practical considerations as this. Nevertheless, his plan (Fig. 72) is not unworkable and it is much more lucid than Street's. There is no great central hall but in the middle is a sort of castle with a huge vaulted hall for the judges to assemble in (Fig. 73). From this, long narrow corridors supported on spidery iron arches fly across the adjoining courtyards to join more corridors communicating with the courts which are massed along the sides of an inner rectangle. Symbolically, it is admirable: the judges massed in their inner citadel then proceeding on their long journeys to administer justice all round them. But it was not thought very practical. Burges's elevations, however, were admitted to be, even by Scott, the most remarkable of any. His whole design is a most exquisite

thing, conceived in the style and spirit of French military and domestic architecture of the twelfth century. It looks, in the airview (Fig. 71), like an enormously elaborated and enriched version of the reconstructed castle in Viollet-le-Duc's article under "Chateau" in the *Dictionnaire Raisonnée*. It creates an entrancing drama of its own, and it is understandable that of all the designs submitted and exhibited it proved the most infectious. I have Burges's own copy of his report. Into it he has pasted prints of two derivatives. One is the design with which his fellow competitor, Lockwood, won the Bradford Town Hall competition in 1869—a really shameless theft, which was actually built; the other is in Glasgow.

With J. P. Seddon[30] we come to one of the most remarkable designs of all (Figs. 74 to 76). One glance at the plan (Fig. 75) reveals a determination to bring the whole vast program within a firm and indivisible architectural unity. Seddon unreservedly accepted the idea of a hall which should also be an approach corridor to *all* the courts (Fig. 76). It was sanctioned for him not by any medieval precedent but by a modern one, the Crystal Palace. Nevertheless all is in Gothic, in stone and wood. In the roof of this hall corridor was an equally long stretch containing the library; below it were refreshment rooms. At one end of this spine stands the magnificent record tower with a water tower at the other. The offices toward the Strand are treated like a range of gabled houses with a clock tower in the middle, and these are insulated from the traffic by a low communicating gallery. The critics were much attracted to this design but shocked to find that it used up only a part of the site, which other competitors found inadequate.[31] Seddon entered the competition two months late to replace a competitor who had given up and the design was probably rushed. His estimate of over £2,000,000 for a building that was only supposed to cost £750,000 (though this figure was raised in the course of the proceedings) must have quickly put him out of the running. But his design is, I think, the one which appeals most immediately to the modern eye.

Alfred Waterhouse[32] sent in a staggering set of drawings some of which have been preserved and others published. His plan (Fig. 78) resembles Scott's in adopting the idea of an internal street, but he follows the majority of other competitors in seeing the central hall as a long spinal corridor. Waterhouse's corridor hall, however, is very high and flanked on each side by three storeys of consulting rooms with windows looking *into* the hall (Fig. 79). With its semicircular roof of iron and glass the hall reminds one a little of the Crystal Palace but even more of the Galleria Vittorio Emmanuele at Milan, just then begun.[33] Behind the batteries of consulting rooms (and at a higher level than the hall) are the courts. And Waterhouse's plan contains another brave stroke. The central hall he reserved for people with business in the courts, but running across it on the short axis was another hall or pair of halls (he called them "transverse halls") for the general public (Fig. 80). The floors of these were at a lower level than the central hall but their vaults opened into it. Where the lower hall crossed the upper hall it was vaultless and open, the upper hall floor crossing it by a narrow bridge. The whole arrangement was reminiscent of a railway cutting between two tunnels, crossed by a footbridge.

To a brilliantly composed piece of three-dimensional planning, Waterhouse added a Strand elevation (Fig. 77) which seems an unnecessarily confused combination of towers and flat surfaces, with a projecting entrance piece like a church west front. He called his style "Early English" but nobody else did. It is rather what Professor Kerr might have called "latitudinarian," the details being described sarcastically by the *Athenaeum's* critic as "the best examples of drawing-room Gothic we have seen."[34] Waterhouse had not the real interest in styles. In this matter he was very soon to go his own hardhearted way while remaining the most ingenious and masterly of Victorian planners.

E. M. Barry,[35] like Scott and Waterhouse, went for the "internal street" idea (Fig. 82) and, like Scott, proposed a central hall (for judges and barristers only, however). This hall was to rise into a cathedral dome which, far from being wasteful, was to be stuffed with records. The courts form a rectangle round this inner core whence they are approached by a series of straight and diagonal bridges. E. M. Barry was, of course, a son of Sir Charles, and his Strand front (Fig. 81) is close in spirit to the River front at Westminster. There is a new sort of "Big Ben" clock tower on the right, and the central dome is very much what James Fergusson said Sir Charles should have placed over his central hall at Westminster.[36] The son even adopts his father's late style of Gothic, a choice which he should have known would go against him in 1866.

Of three designs I have made no mention. H. R. Abraham's[37] plan was a grotesquely articulated disposition of awkward shapes. T. N. Deane's[38] design was pathetic, at least in its externals, which were in the nature of a ludicrously ornate version of his dead partner's (Woodward's) Oxford Museum. H. B. Garling[39] had the worst plan of any, a mere mechanical packaging of the accommodation specified in the program. The fact that he had come out top in the War Office competition of 1857 was evidently no certificate of talent.

After reviewing this battle of giants it is very natural to ask the question: "Who won?" It can never be satisfactorily answered, because it was never satisfactorily decided nor was any one of these designs built.

The designs were judged by a board consisting entirely of laymen with two hardheaded professionals to assist them. The judges were the Chief Commissioner of Works (W. F. Cowper), the Chancellor of the Exchequer (W. E. Gladstone), the Lord Chief Justice (Sir Alexander Cockburn), the lately retired Attorney-General (Sir Roundell Palmer), and a virtuoso M.P. in the person of Sir William Stirling-Maxwell. The professionals were John Shaw and George Pownall, the former an architect of considerable ability. The heads of the law offices were also consulted. Staffs of clerks and draughtsmen were employed to check each design in the greatest possible detail, and in due course two recommendations came before the board of judges. The professionals, Shaw and Pownall, gave the highest number of marks to E. M. Barry and the second highest to Scott. The law officers on the other hand put Scott first and Waterhouse second. On this score Scott might well have expected to repeat, with greater justice, his climbing act of ten years earlier. This did not happen. The judges accepted that Barry had produced the best plan, but they disliked his architecture (alas! for his choice of late Gothic). They therefore recommended to the Treasury that he should be appointed in association with another competitor whose architecture they did like, and their choice fell neither upon Scott nor upon Waterhouse, but on George Edmund Street. The Treasury demurred. Scott and others protested at the injustice. Bitter wrangling ensued, Scott retired hurt, and in June, 1868, the appointment of a single architect was announced. It was Street. Barry was given as a consolation prize the prospect of partly rebuilding the National Gallery. Waterhouse, in due course, was given the Natural History Museum in South Kensington where the thought he had given to the Strand front of his Law Courts design was by no means wasted.

It was never pretended that Street won the competition. But he certainly obtained the commission. The view of the authorities (who included, let us remember, the Lord Chief Justice himself) would be simply this. The architects had joined in a competition with a guaranteed fee of £800 but no guarantee of professional assessment. The judges did, indeed, take professional advice, but having taken it they ignored whole volumes of costly work which proved, in effect, the inconvenience of Street's plan, and appointed him—the man they fancied. Unethical perhaps, but not illegal.

Street's design, in the form in which he submitted it, was never built. Soon after his appointment a diversion occurred in a serious proposal to abandon the Strand site and go to the Embankment. Street made sketches for this site (at Howard Street).[40] In 1871, however, he was back in the Strand but now with a greatly curtailed area to deal with, involving total replanning. His new plan (Fig. 85) was a radical simplification of the first. His hall, instead of being a long double-aisled corridor buried deep in the building became a public hall entered directly from the Strand at its southern end. It stands today, a technically perfect work by an unquestionably great master (Fig. 83). The Record Tower was omitted, with all other towers except a clock tower at the southeast and a ventilation tower on Carey Street. The new exterior design (Fig. 84) is as totally incoherent as the great hall is eloquent. It represents the pathetic collapse of an overstrained imagination. It was ferociously criticized, notably by James Fergusson and E. W. Pugin. Tenders were submitted in 1873 and a contract for £680,000 signed with the contractor, Bull: a wretched sum compared with the 1½ million which would have been the figure for the original design. A hostile and arrogant First Commissioner of Works, Acton Ayrton, worked against Street and his design, tried to eliminate the great hall, and succeeded in lowering the tower. Street faced his troubles with characteristic energy, but when he died in 1881 it was generally felt that the Royal Courts of Justice had destroyed him.

At this point I want to put the whole of this story, for one moment, into a European perspective. It happens that in the very year of the Law Courts competition in London another Law Courts building was begun. This was in Brussels, the capital of a small nation whose political independence was barely a generation old. Nevertheless, Joseph Poelaert's Palais de Justice is probably the biggest thing of its kind ever built.[41] To place the plan of this building (Fig. 86) beside the plan of Street's executed building is to make, even rather ludicrously, one or two points about English architecture in the sixties. The first point is the obvious one that English governments in the mid-nineteenth century were parsimonious to an almost unbelievable degree; their parsimony being part of a national philosophy which expressed itself from time to time in a horrified contempt for architects and architecture. The second point is the astonishing insularity of Victorian architecture. Here it is fair to compare Poelaert's design with Street's as first submitted. Poelaert provided for 27 courts, Street for 24. Poelaert's building cost the equivalent of £1,760,000. Street's was estimated to cost £1,500,000 but would doubtless have cost more. Poelaert's design is a direct and natural product of a tradition deriving from Paris and acknowledged all over the world except, apparently, in London. Street's attaches to no tradition and is utterly unique to London. Placing Poelaert among our eleven London contestants, how does he look? He looks powerful, accomplished, worldly, the confident heir of a great tradition. He is a superb example of success.

If it were my intention to bring this book to a close with a maximum emphasis on the theme of failure with which I began I could hardly, I suppose, have chosen a more shattering conclusion than this tragic story of Street and the Law Courts. But in that particular failure there were extraneous elements, notably administrative vacillation (not to say irresponsibility) and official parsimony. In the competition designs, where eleven architects were given impressive scope for the play of genius, we have a much fairer opportunity of evaluating the power and the weakness of mid-Victorian architecture. Both seem to me to be inextricably involved in this preoccupation with the idea of style to which I have referred so often—this matter of *choice* not only of style, but choice of what components constitute a style and the ambiguity implicit in the obligation to choose. Every design is clearly dominated by this obsession, notwithstanding the absolutely flat refusal of authority to make any obeisance to art in assessing the results. But in the end, as we have seen, even authority itself was seduced by the style-laden pencil of Street. The latent power in the best of the competitors is, I think, unarguable. There is more than a vestige of it in the breathtaking splendor of Street's great hall as actually completed. Seddon's design seems to me one that very nearly broke through the mists of ambiguity to a sense of relationships, independent of style. Waterhouse has some fine strokes. But then Burges conjures up a beautiful twelfth-century vision bordering on the totally absurd. Brandon is totally absurd. Scott, E. M. Barry, and Lockwood cannot liberate themselves, however hard they try, from the Neoclassical tradition which bred them. Nowhere is there any firm common ground. And what we see portrayed in this array of paper architecture is what we find throughout the whole mid-Victorian achievement.

I return to the theme which I proposed in my first lecture, the theme of doubt, of the hectic and arduous pursuit of ideals which were totally incompatible: the desire, on the one hand, to possess a contemporary style and the conviction, on the other, that style meant ornament and that ornament had to be won from the past.

Looking back across a hundred years—and looking back from, of all places, New York—I see the crisis of Victorianism in architecture in the sharpest possible relief. Was this crisis ever resolved? I don't think it was; it was merely forgotten. The twentieth century made the discovery that amid a welter of failure only one Victorian building was a total and absolute success: the Crystal Palace, a structure not designed by an architect and unstigmatized by style. In due course this building was upended, rocketed skywards, and called the Seagram Building; and another great success was scored. The rest of the Victorian world of architecture became concentrated in profound obscurity—a Pandora's box which now seems to be reopening before our eyes. When Pandora was vested by the gods one of her attributes was, I firmly believe, a Ph.D. in the History of Art. Whether this renders the opening of the fatal box more dangerous or less so, the future must decide.

Notes

I. THE EVALUATION OF VICTORIAN ARCHITECTURE

1. G. K. Chesterton, *G. F. Watts* (1904), p. 3.

2. G. M. Trevelyan, *English Social History*, 3rd ed. (1946), p. 524.

3. H. House, "The Mood of Doubt," *Ideas and Beliefs of the Victorians* (1949), pp. 71–77.

4. Article in *D.N.B.* and references there given. J. Summerson, *The Architectural Association, 1847–1947* (1947), pp. 3–10. There is no bibliography of Kerr's writings, most of which are embedded in architectural periodicals and are sometimes anonymous. He wrote on many aspects of theory, construction, and professional practice with which we are not here concerned. The following are the writings which best demonstrate his changing critical attitudes over the years: *Newleafe Discourses on the Fine Art, Architecture* (1846); "The Present Low State of Architectural Education," read to the Association of Architectural Draughtsmen, *Builder*, 1847, pp 58–59; "On Architectural Style," read to the Architectural Association, *ibid.*, pp. 335–36; "The Education of the Architect," read to the Architectural Association, *ibid.*, pp. 491–92; "On the Architecture of the Greeks," read to the Architectural Association, *Builder*, 1848, p. 15; "Remarks on Prof. Donaldson's 'Architectural Maxims and Theorems,'" read to the Architectural Association, *ibid.*, p. 265; "Seven Other Lamps of Architecture," *Builder*, 1851, pp. 710, 731, 764, 780, *ibid.*, 1852, pp. 3, 50, 148, and 178; "The Battle of the Styles," read at the Architectural Exhibition, *Builder*, 1860, pp. 292–94; *The English Gentleman's House* (1865); "Development of the Theory of the Architecturesque," *R.I.B.A. Sessional Papers*, 1st ser., vol. 19 (1868–69), pp. 89–104; "The Position

of the Architectural Profession," read at the Conference of Architects, 1874, *Builder*, 1874, pp. 529–30; "The Treatment of Scientific Engineering Artistically," read to the Architectural Association, *Builder*, 1876, p. 235; "English Architecture Thirty Years Hence," *R.I.B.A. Transactions*, 1st ser., vol. 34 (1883–84), pp. 218–30; "Ruskin and Emotional Architecture," *R.I.B.A. Journal*, vol. vii (1900), p. 181; chap. 6 in vol. ii of J. Fergusson, *History of the Modern Styles of Architecture*, 3rd ed. (1891).

5. In his writings of this period, Kerr gives expression to two associated ideas which had been present in English architectural theory for some time. The first is the potentiality of imaginative freedom in architecture; the second is the idea of a contemporary architecture. For discussion of the earlier development of these ideas see S. Lang, "Richard Payne Knight and the Idea of Modernity," *Concerning Architecture: Essays presented to Nikolaus Pevsner* (ed. J. Summerson; 1968) and P. Collins, *Changing Ideals in Modern Architecture* (1965), chap. 13. The idea of a contemporary architecture tends to take two forms: (a) an eclectic combination of features from existing styles and (b) an entirely new style based on new materials and circumstances. After his initial pleas for imaginative freedom, Kerr aligns himself with the latter. With the idea of a contemporary architecture comes the idea that architecture "reflects the character of the time," and this leads to the further idea that any new architecture *should* reflect that character. In his paper of 1869, quoted later, Kerr calls this reflection of character the "essential attribute" of architecture.

6. *Builder*, 1860, pp. 292–94.

7. C. F. Hayward, "Modernism in Art," *Building News*, 1860, pp. 275–76. Hayward calls the reading room of the British Museum "a piece of real modernism."

8. *Building News*, 1857, p. 119.

9. National Provident Institution, Gracechurch Street, 1857 (*Builder*, 1863, pp. 11–13); houses at Westerham (*ibid.*, 1863, pp. 442–43), Ascot Heath (*ibid.*, 1868, pp. 928–29), and Lingfield (*ibid.*, 1869, pp. 1025–27).

10. *R.I.B.A. Sessional Papers*, 1st ser., vol. 19 (1868–69), p. 104.

11. J. T. Emmett, "The State of English Architecture," *Quarterly Review*, vol. 132, no. 264 (1872). At an architects' conference in 1872, T. H. Wyatt, President of the R.I.B.A., mentioned an attack on English architects in "the most influential of our daily journals." He was probably referring to E. W. Pugin's letter, *Times*, May 7, 1872, p. 47.

12. For the abolition of Pennethorne's office and the "reform"

of the Office of Works under Acton Smee Ayrton, as First Commissioner, see *Builder*, 1877, p. 897 *et seq.*

13. *Fifty Years of Public Work of Sir Henry Cole* (1884), vol. ii, pp. 296, 305.

14. A. E. Street, *Memoir of G. E. Street* (1888), pp. 158–66.

15. *The Works of John Ruskin* (ed. E. T. Cook and A. Wedderburn; 1902–12), vol. 23 p. xli; vol. 34, p. 513 (Ruskin's letter).

16. *Builder*, 1872, p. 860.

17. *Builder*, 1873, p. 202. "That is the modern European manner from which we have gone away and to which we must return."

18. J. Fergusson, *History of the Modern Styles of Architecture* (1891), p. 123. See also Kerr's estimate of Ruskin in the obituary tribute, "Ruskin and Emotional Architecture," *R.I.B.A. Journal*, vol. vii (1900), pp. 181 *et seq.*

19. *Die Neuere Kirchliche Baukunst in England* (Berlin, 1901).

20. *Das Englische Haus* (Berlin, 1908–10).

21. A biographical article by the present writer will appear in the volume of the *D.N.B.* for 1950–59.

22. *Vitruvian Nights: Papers upon Architectural Subjects* (1932); *English Architecture Since the Regency* (1953).

23. *First and Last Loves* (1952), a book of essays mainly on Victorian architecture, is a possible exception.

II. TWO VICTORIAN STATIONS

1. London County Council, *Survey of London*, vol. xxi (1949) (St. Pancras, part 3), pp. 107–14.

2. C. L. V. Meeks, *The Railway Station: an Architectural History* (1957), p. 45, figs. 13 and 20.

3. E. Course, *London Railways* (1962), chap. 1. *Companion to the Almanac*, 1844, pp. 239–41. The view reproduced here is in the R.I.B.A. library.

4. Shortly to be demolished. Photographs in National Monuments Record.

5. *Illustrated London News*, May 4, 1844, p. 284. Meeks, *op. cit.*, pp. 38 and 46.

6. H. R. Hitchcock, *Early Victorian Architecture* (1954), pp. 432–33 and plate xiii, 20.

7. London County Council, *Survey of London*, vol. xxiv (St. Pancras, part 4), pp. 115–16. C. H. Grinling, *The History of the Great Northern Railway* (1898), p. 114. *Builder*, 1851, p. 739; *ibid.*, 1852,

pp. 625 *et seq.* Meeks, *op. cit.*, compares King's Cross with the exactly contemporary Gare Montparnasse, Paris, by Victor Lenoir with shed by Flachat. The French facade seems to rely on Cubitt's original design but is more architecturally developed. Flachat's shed has flat roofs.

8. Meeks, *op. cit.*, p. 59; fig. 44.

9. E. Kaufmann, *Architecture in the Age of Reason* (1955), pp. 213–14.

10. Hitchcock, *op. cit.*, p. 534; plate xvi, i.

11. Architectural Publication Society, *Dictionary of Architecture*, s.v. "Bent Timber."

12. A. T. Walmisley, *Iron Roofs: examples of Design* (1884; 2nd ed., 1888), plate 52.

13. Compare the design for a Bourse in J. N. L. Durand, *Precis des Lecons* (1802), vol. ii, plate 14.

14. J. Fergusson, *History of the Modern Styles of Architecture* (1862), pp. 479–80.

15. Vol. 132, no. 264 (1872), pp. 295 *et seq.*

16. H. R. Hitchcock, "Brunel and Paddington," *Architectural Review,* 1951, pp. 240–46. *Illustrated London News,* December 18, 1852, pp. 537–38; *ibid.,* July 8, 1854, pp. 13–14; *ibid.,* September 2, 1854, p. 217. *Companion to the Almanac,* 1853, pp. 252–53. Perspective drawings of the hotel in R.I.B.A. library.

17. *Illustrated London News,* July 8, 1854, p. 14.

18. *Builder,* 1860, p. 755.

19. Meeks, *op. cit.*, p. 93.

20. What follows is based on the two histories of the Midland Railway: F. S. Williams, *The Midland Railway: its Rise and Progress* (5th ed. 1886) and C. E. Stretton, *The History of the Midland Railway* (1901). See also *Building News,* 1869, pp. 136 and 274.

21. Walmisley, *op. cit.*, plates 53–56. *Building News,* 1869, p. 136.

22. Meeks, *op. cit.*, p. 88.

23. *Builder,* 1865, p. 897.

24. *Builder,* 1866, p. 105.

25. G. Gilbert Scott, *Personal and Professional Recollections* (1879), pp. 721–72.

26. See p. 00 and Fig. 00.

27. Scott, *op. cit.*, p. 271.

28. "The State of English Architecture," *Quarterly Review,* vol. 132, no. 264., pp. 295 *et seq.*

29. Scott, *loc. cit.*

30. *History of the Modern Styles, loc. cit.*

III. TWO LONDON CHURCHES

1. Article in *D.N.B.* There is a memorial tablet to the Misses Monk in St. James's church.

2. I am indebted to Sir Philip Magnus-Allcroft, Bt., for information about his wife's grandfather.

3. *Dod's Parliamentary Companion* (1880), p. 161.

4. Article in *D.N.B.*

5. Lamb wrote a *Memoir of the late J. C. Loudon, Esq.,* read before the R.I.B.A., on December 18, 1843, the MS. of which is in the R.I.B.A. library.

6. *Builder,* 1869, p. 720.

7. A. E. Street, *Memoir of George Edmund Street, R. A.* (1888).

8. *Ecclesiologist,* vol. xix (1861), p. 317.

9. *Stones of Venice,* chap. xix, sec. 12.

10. *Companion to the Almanac,* 1862, p. 252.

11. *Building News,* August 9, 1861, pp. 663–64.

12. *Ecclesiologist, loc. cit.*

13. *Illustrated London News,* February 1, 1862, p. 121. *Companion to the Almanac, loc. cit.*

14. The fresco deteriorated and by 1903 had been replaced by the present mosaic. H. Macmillan, *G. F. Watts* (1903), pp. 51–52.

15. J. T. Emmet in "The State of English Architecture," *Quarterly Review,* vol. 132, no. 264, p. 295, calls it a "baby house."

16. *Builder,* October 20, 1866, pp. 778–81.

17. *Studies of Ancient Domestic Architecture principally selected from original drawings in the collection of the late Sir William Burrell Bt., with some brief observations on the application of ancient architecture to the pictorial composition of Modern Edifices* (1846), p. 3.

18. *Ibid.,* p. 5.

19. *Ibid.,* p. 3.

20. *Builder,* October 20, 1866, p. 781.

21. Some of the glass was perhaps designed by Lamb. There are six designs for glass by him in the Victoria and Albert Museum (C.G. 66/9246).

22. *Loc. cit.*

23. *Companion to the Almanac,* 1866, pp. 153–54 and 1867, pp. 147–48.

24. *Ecclesiologist,* 1855, p. 150.

25. *Ibid.,* 1850, p. 172.

26. *R.I.B.A. Journal,* April, 1949, p. 251.

27. N. Pevsner, *London except the Cities of London and West-minster* (1952), p. 360.

IV. A VICTORIAN COMPETITION

1. A. Barry, *The Life and Works of Sir. C. Barry* (1863), chaps. vi and vii. H. T. Ryde, *Illustrations of the New Palace of Westminster* (1849; 2nd series, 1865).

2. "We have no hesitation in giving it as our opinion, that the Elevations are of an order so superior, and display so much taste and knowledge of Gothic Architecture, as to leave no doubt whatever in our minds of the Author's ability to carry into effect Your Majesty's Commands." *Report of Commissioners appointed to consider the Plans for Building the Houses of Parliament (Reports from Commissioners,* 1836, vol. xxxvi).

3. "The Story of the Government Offices," *Builder,* 1877, pp. 852 *et seq.*

4. *Illustrated London News,* vol. 31 (1857), pp. 100–1. *Builder,* 1857, p. 434. *Building News,* 1857, p. 854.

5. *Illustrated London News,* vol. 31 (1857), pp. 148–49. *Builder,* 1857, p. 435. *Building News,* 1857, p. 959.

6. *Illustrated London News,* vol. 31 (1857), pp. 228–29. *Builder,* 1857, pp. 450–51.

7. *Illustrated London News,* vol. 31 (1857), pp. 348–49.

8. *Illustrated London News,* vol. 31 (1857), p. 349. Original drawing in R.I.B.A. Library.

9. *Illustrated London News,* vol. 31 (1857), p. 412.

10. *Builder,* 1855, p. 319. C. L. Eastlake, *A History of the Gothic Revival* (1872), pp. 283–87. K. Clark, *The Gothic Revival* (revised ed., 1950), pp. 282–87.

11. Scott's plans and perspectives are in the R.I.B.A. Library. They contain variations, however, from the competition designs engraved in *Builder,* 1857, p. 495, and *Building News,* 1857, p. 855.

12. G. Gilbert Scott, *Personal and Professional Recollections* (1879), p. 178.

13. *Illustrated London News,* vol. 31 (1857), p. 348.

14. *Builder,* 1857, p. 563.

15. "A most notable design for sheltering the war council of the nation." *Building News,* 1857, p. 613. Ruskin disclaimed any share in the design. *Builder,* 1857, p. 283.

16. *Illustrated London News,* vol. 31 (1857), p. 412.

17. *Building News,* 1857, p. 129.

18. *Builder,* 1857, p. 370.

19. *Illustrated London News,* vol. 31 (1857), p. 276. *Builder,* 1857, p. 479.

20. Scott's side of the story is told in *Personal and Professional Recollections,* pp. 178–201. For the relevant debates in the House of Commons see Hansard, vols. cl (May 28, 1858) and clii (February 11 and 18, 1859).

21. *Builder,* 1859, pp. 328–29; 1865, pp. 136–37. Eastlake, *op. cit.,* p. 312–25.

22. A. E. Street, *Memoir of G. E. Street* (1888), chap. 8. An article by M. H. Port will appear in the forthcoming vol. 10 of *Architectural History.*

23. The designs are reviewed at length in *Builder,* 1867, p. 69. The *Building News,* 1867, contains a series of critical articles on the designs, as follows: p. 18 (possible types of plan), p. 57 (the competitors), p. 79 (Scott), p. 95 (Waterhouse), p. 117 (Street), p. 137 (Seddon), p. 153 (Lockwood), p. 169 (Garling), p. 186 (Deane), p. 202 (Burges), p. 219 (Brandon), p. 234 (E. M. Barry and H. R. Abraham), p. 249 (conclusion). The *Athenaeum,* 1867, vol. i, contains critical articles at pp. 125, 162, 227, 258, and 327. See also *Spectator,* February 23, 1867. An article in *Westminster Gazette* is reprinted in *Building News,* 1867, p. 197, and in the same volume are reviews of press comments generally (p. 413) and an article in the *Quarterly Review* (p. 515). The reports of all the competitors were printed with floor plans and, in some cases, photographs of elevations and perspectives.

24. 1811–78. The only biography is his own *Personal and Professional Recollections,* edited by his son, G. Gilbert Scott (1879). Article in *D.N.B.* and references there given. K. Clark, *The Gothic Revival* (1928; 2nd ed., 1950), Chap. IX.

25. See, for example, J. N. L. Durand, *Precis des Lecons,* vol. 1, plate 8.

26. 1811–78. Obituary in *Builder,* July 27, 1878, p. 788. Born in Doncaster, he was articled to the younger Peter Atkinson of York. He started practice in Hull but moved to Bradford in 1849 where he built the Town Hall, markets, St. George's Hall and Exchange. He moved to London in 1874 and built the City Temple and the Inns of Court Hotel.

27. 1817–77. Obituary in *Building News,* October 12, 1877, pp. 369–70. Pupil of J. Dedeau of Alencon who had studied under Huyot, and later of J. T. Parkinson of London. His Catholic Apostolic church,

Gordon Square (1851–55), is an Early English work of great virtuosity. He wrote, with his brother, J. A. Brandon, the *Analysis of Gothic Architecture* (1847) and, after his brother's death, *Parish Churches* (1848) and *Open Timber Roofs* (1849). A man of psychopathic scrupulousness, he became an alcoholic and committed suicide.

28. 1824–81. *Memoir of George Edmund Street* (1888) by his son, A. E. Street. Article in *D.N.B.* and references there given. H. S. Goodhart-Rendel, "George Edmund Street," *Builder,* April 3, 1953, p. 519. J. Kinnard, "G. E. Street, the Law Courts and the 'Seventies,'" *Victorian Architecture* (ed. P. Ferriday, 1963).

29. 1827–81. Article in *D.N.B.* and references there given. Charles Handley-Read, "William Burges," *Victorian Architecture* (ed. P. Ferriday, 1963). *The Architectural Designs of William Burges* (ed. R. P. Pullan, 1883); second series (Stonework), 1887.

30. 1827–1906. Article in *D.N.B.,* and references there given. Obituary in *Builder,* February 13, 1906.

31. 1867, p. 391, etc.

32. 1830–1905. Article in *D.N.B.* and references there given. Obituary in *Builder,* August 26, 1905, p. 237.

33. H. R. Hitchcock, *Architecture: Nineteenth and Twentieth Centuries* (Pelican History of Art, 1958), pp. 146–47, plate 75B. The gallery was built by an English firm, and Matthew Digby Wyatt was on the English board.

34. 1867, p. 391, etc.

35. 1830–80. Memoir by Rev. Alfred Barry in E. M. Barry, *Lectures on Architecture* (1881). Article in *D.N.B.*

36. J. Fergusson, *History of the Modern Styles of Architecture* (1862), p. 325.

37. Abraham was a son of Robert Abraham (1774–1850), architect. His principal work was the Middle Temple Library, a competent piece of Decorated Gothic, destroyed by bombs in 1941. He played an important part in the formation of Victoria Street.

38. 1828–99. Son of Sir Thomas Deane. Article in *D.N.B.* and references there given. Both the elder and the younger Deanes worked in partnership with Benjamin Woodward up to his death in 1861.

39. 1821 or 1822–1909. He won the War Office competition in 1856, competed for the Law Courts in 1866 and the Admiralty in 1885, and made a new design for a War Office in 1889, but no public building of his was ever built.

40. *Architect,* June 12, 1869, pp. 306–8. *Building News,* May 5, 1871 (supplement).

41. J. Poelaert, *Le Nouveau Palais de Justice de Bruxelles* [1904].

Index